Hustling Ve

"*Hustling Verse* marks a profound shift in Canadian letters. We have left the centre for the periphery. In the periphery there is a shared understanding that the poetic desire is firstly a desire to remake the world for those tailgated by structural violence of all kinds. Justin Ducharme and Amber Dawn's curatorial efforts amount on the one hand to a scathing critique of white supremacist cisheteropatriachal capitalism and the long marginalization of art by and for sex workers and on the other to a resounding refusal of the old way of being a poet in Canada."
—Billy-Ray Belcourt, author of *This Wound Is a World*

"*Hustling Verse* is a book of incantations that crackle with urgency and power. The span of these poems covers enormous ground while remaining united by an unwavering commitment to speaking the truth in all its painful and healing beauty."
—Kai Cheng Thom, author of *Fierce Femmes and Notorious Liars*

"Each poem, an intricate, beautiful, sometimes haunting room we are invited into, to listen, pay attention, learn something. *Hustling Verse* is not only an important addition to the landscape of literature, it's a necessity."
—Daniel Zomparelli, founder of *Poetry Is Dead* magazine

"Curated with care and compassion, *Hustling Verse* is a book about economies of care and cruelty, of wounding and warning and wonder. This is so much more than a book with a social message— it's beautiful, heartrending, nourishing truth, one that so perfectly embodies the transformative power of poetry at its very best."
—Daniel Heath Justice, author of *Why Indigenous Literatures Matter*

HUSTLING
Verse

HUSTLING

An Anthology of Sex Workers' Poetry

Edited by Amber Dawn and Justin Ducharme

verse

ARSENAL PULP PRESS
VANCOUVER

HUSTLING VERSE
Copyright © 2019 by Amber Dawn and Justin Ducharme
Foreword copyright © 2019 by Mercedes Eng
Poems copyright © 2019 by individual contributors

THIRD PRINTING: 2023

ARSENAL PULP PRESS
Suite 202 – 211 East Georgia St.
Vancouver, BC V6A 1Z6
Canada
arsenalpulp.com

The publisher gratefully acknowledges the support of the Canada Council for the Arts and the British Columbia Arts Council for its publishing program, and the Government of Canada, and the Government of British Columbia (through the Book Publishing Tax Credit Program), for its publishing activities.

Arsenal Pulp Press acknowledges the xʷməθkʷəy̓əm (Musqueam), Sḵwx̱wú7mesh (Squamish), and səl̓ilwətaʔɬ (Tsleil-Waututh) Nations, speakers of Hul'q'umi'num'/Halq'eméylem/həńq̓əmińəḿəńq custodians of the traditional, ancestral, and unceded territories where our office is located. We pay respect to their histories, traditions, and continuous living cultures and commit to accountability, respectful relations, and friendship.

Cover and text design by Oliver McPartlin
Cover illustration by Exotic Cancer
Copy edited by Doretta Lau
Proofread by Alison Strobel and Jaiden Dembo

Printed and bound in Canada

Library and Archives Canada Cataloguing in Publication:
Hustling verse : an anthology of sex workers' poetry / edited by Amber Dawn and Justin Ducharme.
Other titles: Anthology of sex workers' poetry
Names: Dawn, Amber, 1974- editor. | Ducharme, Justin, 1994- editor.
Description: Poetry.
Identifiers: Canadiana (print) 20190121130 | Canadiana (ebook) 20190127120 | ISBN 9781551527819 (softcover) | ISBN 9781551527826 (HTML)
Subjects: LCSH: Prostitution—Poetry. | LCSH: Sex workers—Poetry. | LCSH: Poetry—21st century.
Classification: LCC PN6101 .H87 2019 | DDC 811/.608092130674—dc23

To every brilliant sex worker, most especially to those who've been denied their shine and truth

CONTENTS

Foreword

It is an honour to have my poem seeded in *Hustling Verse: An Anthology of Sex Workers' Poetry* amongst so many beautiful poems. It is a gift and a responsibility to write a foreword for this collectively dreamed space, conjured by coeditors Amber Dawn and Justin Ducharme. I can't imagine what it would have been like to have access to a book like this years ago, when I was in recovery from heroin addiction and still carrying a lot of shame about having worked in the sex trade. In recovery, my heroines were empowered women of colour like T-Boz, Chilli, and Left Eye of the all-girl R&B group TLC—women who owned their melanin and their sexual desires and didn't let anybody fuck with them. But books like *Hustling Verse*, like Amber Dawn's *How Poetry Saved My Life: A Hustler's Memoir*—books written by sex workers that didn't position us as one-dimensional and disempowered—hadn't yet been published, nor had *Mercenary English*, a book of poetry about my time in the survival sex trade in Vancouver's Downtown Eastside (DTES).

When I first heard TLC I was titties deep into addiction, and by the time I got clean, the group's stunna MC Lisa "Left Eye" Lopes was dead, like so many of the women I worked with, except their deaths weren't accidents like hers. Then I left the trade, and TLC's "Unpretty" was my favourite recovery song. I felt unpretty as a mixed-race girl of Chinese and settler descent, coded as an Indigenous person, growing up in the Prairies, where white supremacy reigns. I felt unpretty because I had been a ho, a woman who "sold" what society teaches women is their most valuable asset: their sexuality. At detox, one aspect of recovery we addressed through art therapy—for those of us who were feeling some type of way but didn't have words to talk about it—was low self-esteem and body image. I formed clay to spell out "UNPRETTY" in capital letters, and after they dried, I threw them into rushing glacial waters that flow through the unceded territories of the xʷməθkʷəy̓əm (Musqueam), Sḵwx̱wú7mesh (Squamish), and səl̓ilwətaʔɬ (Tsleil-Waututh) Nations, asking to be free of the bullshit idea that I wasn't absolutely perfect as is.

But it was difficult to get free of white supremacy and heteropatriarchy, the idea that I was always already less valuable than other people because I was a person of colour, a woman, and "used goods," so I looked to writing as a way of healing and working though shame I felt for having sex-worked. Sex workers are a stigmatized population, and dominant society repeatedly tells us that we are disposable. When I worked low track in the DTES in the mid-1990s, a staggering number of women from the area were disappeared and murdered while the police did nothing. How else could I feel when the deaths of my sisters were acceptable to the police and the public? It's so clear to me now who ought to be ashamed.

Writing was also a way to cultivate my anger when it emerged, because after dispelling the shame, the anger came. Anger at the police/RCMP for doing nothing; at the public who limit their perception of sex workers to stereotypes such as trafficked sex slaves who need to be rescued or addicts and disease carriers culpable for any violence enacted against them because of their "lifestyle choices"; at the media that reinforces these racist stereotypes while ignoring the effects of colonization and racism, the same media that immediately began sensationalizing the gruesome details of the murders once the police finally acted. And lastly, anger at being researched and written about by people who are not sex workers. Anger helped me birth *Mercenary English* in 2013, and her first words were "nothing about us without us."

The poem I contributed to *Hustling Verse* was originally published in *M'aidez*, a chapbook on labour organized by Press Release, a writing collective that coalesced around the anti-Olympics movement. *M'aidez* dropped May 1, 2012, on International Workers' Day, in solidarity with student uprisings and calls for general strikes across Turtle Island. In 2012, my many years of struggling to pay for university classes through shitty minimum-wage jobs finally paid off and I got a teaching job as a sessional at a small college, joining the "precarious cognitive labour classes," a phrase I learned in grad school. I'm still a sessional, but I make more money than I've ever made. Often, I feel guilty about the money, about the privilege and ease it allows, and how easily I can spend it. It's unexpected, this guilt that I realize is survivor's guilt. Through writing this foreword I also realize I'm still in survival mode, though that is no longer my situation. Thank you to the coeditors and all the contributors of *Hustling Verse* for creating this healing space.

My experience was of the survival sex trade, but sex work exists on a spectrum, as modalities of sex work are many and mutable, as are we sex workers. This is why *Hustling Verse* is so important: gathered here are multiple narratives of our lived experiences and the contexts that gave rise to our experiences. We are not abject victims without agency, even though sex workers are often victims of violence. Justin Ducharme and Akira the Hustler's poems show that we are affective labourers providing tenderness, healers giving medicine. Naomi Sayer's poem illuminates how the remote locations where some Indigenous sex workers live makes getting to and from work dangerous, and that the public would wrongly view her father as a human trafficker because he drives her to the strip club where she chooses to work, though he does so to ensure she arrives safely.

Sex workers are protectors of ourselves and our friends, and our chosen and blood fams protect us. We are astute analysts of the media, language, legislation, labour, beauty standards, homophobia, transphobia, colonization, and racism. And we are poets.

AMBER DAWN

Every Time a Sex Worker Is Written about in an Institutional Form, a Poem Dies

How Poetry Saved My Life: A Hustler's Memoir first launched at a crowded jazz pub in Vancouver's Downtown Eastside on April 12, 2013, and on that night I became one of a very few sex workers with a published poetry collection and/or a poetry-memoir hybrid. Six years later, if you Google search "poetry + sex work" (from a North American location) my name still comes up as one of the top and most common results.

To me, this is both predictable and preposterous.

It is predictable because sex workers are denied personal agency and expression in nearly every aspect of our lives. The erasure of and stigma surrounding sex work means that routine activities—such as going to a doctor's appointment or making new friends—are risky. Self-censorship or complete silence are the only guaranteed means to mitigate the risks.

In *How Poetry Saved My Life*, and in dozens of interviews and articles since, I have stated that criminalization, full or asymmetrical, and other barriers that prevent sex workers from openly expressing ourselves is the very basis of our subjugation. And what subjugates a population even further? Having their "stories" told through power-holding outsiders. Stories in quotation marks, as these narratives and portrayals are largely inaccurate.

In Canada, the nation to which I am a first-generation settler and the site of four hundred plus years of colonial violence, the practice of power-holding outsiders telling inaccurate stories has been and remains intrinsic to the systemic oppression of Indigenous people. Inaccurate stories help charge the destruction of communities, land, resources, and knowledge—and encourage (mainly white) Canadians to perpetuate everyday biases and aggressions toward Indigenous people. Power-holders have long mastered the abuse of stories. The dissemination of inaccurate stories additionally, and intentionally, harms people of colour, immigrants and migrants, trans and queer people, criminalized poor (such as homeless populations), people with disabilities, and sex workers.

Again, in *How Poetry Saved My Life* and in interviews and articles, I've talked about sex workers being among the most researched, debated, and regulated population in Canada, but that we are almost never the leading voices in these studies, debates, or rules. The recent rise in social media as an information source has provided some space for sex workers to voice our own stories, though our stories are heavily banned, censored, and trolled. And in view of the United States bill package FOSTA-SESTA, passed as law by Congress in April 2018, sex workers now have fewer spaces where we can work, connect to clients and colleagues, share stories, and express ourselves. Now as much as ever, our stories are being inaccurately told by power-holding outsiders.

There is a third way that stories and subjugation have been made to work harmfully together. The first time I told my story as a sex worker it was to a social worker. I was a seventeen-year-old runaway and this social worker was determining if and how I was surviving without parental support, and if I would qualify for government assistance. I don't know why exactly I outed myself as an underage sex worker and shared parts of my story. Maybe evoking pity was the strongest, most practised strategy I had at the time. Maybe I was simply a terrified kid who was truly desperate for anyone to see me. What I know now is that this moment—of watching the social worker tick boxes on a form while sliding a box of tissues across her desk at me—clinched a sickly association between telling my story and fear. The memory of the social worker's office is not one I wrote about in *How Poetry Saved My Life*, or in any interviews and articles thereafter. Prior to this introduction, I have only discreetly recounted this memory to other sex workers. And in turn, other sex workers have shared their own memories of fearfully telling parts of their stories to doctors, landlords, police officers, lawyers, and similar authority figures.

It's a triangle of subjugation, really: one point silences sex workers, the second disseminates inaccurate stories told by outsiders, and the third maintains environments of fear during the rare times we are asked for our stories.

It is predictable that sex workers are grossly under-recognized as poets. Every time a sex worker is written about in an institutional form, a poem dies. The pointed ways in which our stories have been mistreated is the opposite of poetry.

Poetry is to dream, desire, resist, emote, express, and create new possibilities. It's likely that you—readers who are poets or poetry lovers yourselves—detect the bright shift in my tone and language as soon as I mention poetry on this page. Now that I've brought poetry in, I can address you directly. I can speak as a fuller version of the "I" that I've been going on about for the last eight hundred words. And what I have to say is every time a sex worker writes a poem, we transcend all the harms that have been done to our stories. Every time a sex worker writes a poem, we rise above subjugation.

Which brings me to the reason why I find it preposterous that I am one of a very few published and recognized sex worker poets. It's preposterous because sex workers are system-smashing-creative-fucking geniuses. You shouldn't be able to throw a whip without hitting a poetry collection written by a sex worker. Truth, and all-caps TRUTH, we're nimble word-and-image smiths. We're highly expressive and engaged performers. We can embody a dozen personas a night. We can spin the five senses into divinity. Our very bodies act as bridges between the mundane and the fantastic. Just read the ad copy for our business hustle and you'll find poetry. Just follow #sexwork on Twitter and you'll find poetry. Just visit the staff room of a club or parlour or porn studio (well, don't, actually, unless you work there) and the workers will be spitting poetry.

I've suspected the connection between sex workers and poetry for a long time. Alongside writing *How Poetry Saved My Life*, I began to develop and facilitate poetry and/or memoir writing workshops specifically for sex workers. I wanted not only to find other sex worker poets; I also wanted us to make meaning and magic together. I'd like to thank the many sex worker organizations and groups that hosted me: In Vancouver, where I live, the WISH Drop-In Centre, the Asian

Society for the Intervention of AIDS (ASIA), PACE Society, Sex Workers United Against Violence (SWUAV), Boys 'R' Us, and the Hooker Monologues; across Canada, Maggie's Toronto and the Sex Workers of Winnipeg Action Coalition (SWWAC); and in the United States, the Red Umbrella Project in New York and the San Francisco Bay Area Sex Workers Film and Arts Festival. Several *Hustling Verse* contributors are poets I met at one of these workshops.

The writing workshops I facilitate are modelled around freewriting prompts and optional sharing, which is not so different from some of the creative writing curriculum I bring to campus classrooms. I do try to tailor the writing prompts to suit sex workers' lived experiences, with the freewrites I call *Shit My Clients Say*, *What Does Your Job Smell Like*, and an adapted version of *Two Truths and a Lie* being three of my more popular exercises. My own poem "The World's Oldest Love Spell (A Fairy Tale)" (p. 193) is the result of a two-hour writing workshop where a group of eight sex workers and I explored themes of our superpowers and/ or mythical selves.

Something that I've found to be unique about writing with sex workers is an exceptional willingness to share. Frequently, after a freewrite each and every writer will read, word for word, what they've written. Sex workers (contrary to what we're forced to believe about ourselves) are not afraid of our own stories. We're not afraid to be messy and raw, to be forthright and unrestrained, and to be expressive as holy fuck. To sit at a table with sex workers reading their first and spontaneous drafted poetry is, I repeat, to rise above subjugation.

My brilliant coeditor, Justin Ducharme, and I were struck by a similar uplifted sensation while reading the two hundred plus submissions we received for this anthology. We knew there would be unflinching and genuinely arousing poems about sex, such as Jasbina Justice's "slippery, sticky, messy, gooey." (p. 82) and jan maudlin's "Playing" (p. 131).

We anticipated humour poems—from slapstick to irony—that would broaden how we think about the overlaps between identity, humour, and craft. We found this vital overlap in Keva I Lee's "Triple F Threat" (p. 158) and jaye simpson's "godzilla (2014)" (p. 83).

We hoped for place-making poems, for a type of embodied verse that would explore the structural relationship between sex workers and their environments. Juba Kalamka's "three different streets" (p. 94) and Naomi Sayers' "A Memory I Need to Talk About" (p. 40) are shining examples of this embodiment.

And, finally, as Justin and I read, we were reminded, again and again, that poems traversing silence, fear, stigma, and trauma are critical to this anthology. And what have these fifty-seven sex worker poets done to acknowledge and transform these harms? This, my dear readers, is a question you might want to ask yourself while reading. Look for Strawberry's "3 strong pairs of hands" (p. 112), which shows how the poet "took my fear and spun it into red wool / that trails behind me so I can find my way back." Look for Pluma Sumaq's "You especially," (p. 51) that reveals "the quiet eruption of underground volcanoes, / the way we were never meant to be seen." Look at every page, stanza, and line and I promise you will witness the many ways that poetry can acknowledge and transform, how poetry can hold and heal.

Thank you for witnessing our poetry. Thank you for being uplifted, with us, and rising above subjugation. Thank you for helping poems be alive.

JUSTIN DUCHARME

Musings on Self-Representation

For as long as I can remember, I've been trying to find pieces of myself in other people. Most of the time, it's been those who look nothing like me or, to my belief, have never experienced certain things the way I did. The blond-haired, blue-eyed boy at school with a seemingly perfect family. That Hollywood filmmaker I really admired growing up. My white girlfriend in high school. Literally anyone whose parents didn't constantly fear child apprehension. This habit I fostered very early on made me hate myself, because the worth and healing that I was searching for was never going to come from those I sought out.

When I was in my late teens, I was taught the importance of self-representation. An elder told me to not wait for someone else to make me feel seen or heard but to find myself through those feelings of uncertainty and sadness. That lesson provided me with an important personal shift, almost jolting me awake to a different way of thinking. It probably also explains my incessant need to provide hypervisibility within my work as a writer and filmmaker. Since committing to my art, I keep in mind the same question—Why search for myself in failed narratives when I can create my own?

> he is
> un touchable, unreadable,
>
> more lovely than smooth gravity
> —"the dancer (club mix)" by Gregory Scofield (p. 29)

When I moved from my tiny hometown on Treaty 1 territory to the big city, there was one thing that became known pretty fucking quickly: I had to grow up. I had come out here to escape a life I thought didn't have room for me to be myself, and I wasn't entirely sure what I wanted or needed to be successful in this relocation. I was going to film school five days a week and receiving a living allowance that was barely covering my East Vancouver rent when I began hustling. In the first year of doing sex work, I didn't tell a soul. This was largely because of the stigma sex workers face from the general public, and from loved ones. Apart from one boy I occasionally worked with, I had no known community with the same lived experience. After an altercation with a speed-hungry daddy in the West End that resulted in a broken hot-pink skateboard deck and a busted lip, I confided in close friends about my whereabouts when I was on the job. I began to feel more comfortable talking about my hustle to my chosen family, which made me safer when working.

We are a proud people. Sex work does not make us weak.
—Sacred Collective (p. 122)

Last year I wrote and directed my third short film, titled *Positions*, about a male Indigiqueer sex worker's day-to-day experience with clients. When it came time to raise funds for the project and find people to collaborate with, it was very important to me that people know this story was, as I called it, "sorta kinda auto-biographical." As a lover of cinema, I know it is very, very rare for someone to capture sex workers onscreen with nuance and agency, and this project was always going to be something that was filling a hole in my moviegoer heart. Coming out as a sex worker who makes art about sex work is interesting. People are very eager to engage with me but are either unsure of how to do that properly or too afraid to even try. Within the first three public screenings of *Positions*, I'd experienced my fair share of stupid questions and invasive inquiries. "Why didn't he just get an actual job?" "Why would he call his grandma right after?" "Why would he still sleep with someone who's just made racist remarks to him?" It's astonishing that people will try to strip you of your agency just because they cannot relate or see you as an actual human being unless they first feel pity. I've come to assume that these people have no idea what it's like to be poor or unemployable.

I made it despite the fact that the world said I shouldn't have
—"I made it" by Sumter (p. 63)

To say that working on this anthology has lifted my spirit would be an understatement. From the get-go, Amber Dawn and I were floored by the overwhelming number of brilliant and creative sex workers who were taking up rightful space in this narrative that should've always been ours to begin with and spitting out expressive poetry to talk about things the way we want to talk about them. When people are given the reins to tell their stories in the way they choose, it has an extreme impact on the way they navigate the world, the way they value themselves. And when stories are told through an experiential point of view, it opens pathways for dialogue—a dialogue that is controlled by the very people it's about. My hope is that *Hustling Verse* opens the doors for all of the creative sex workers whose stories have been gatekept by others and allows them the freedom to explore their lived experience through their art. My own healing journey has benefited from the creation of this anthology, and I hope, too, that it can impart teachings to other workers about self-representation, just like that elder did for me many years ago.

Ultimately, I hope that other workers find themselves within the pages of this anthology and feel home.

Thank you for reading.

JUSTIN DUCHARME

dream boy

I transform for pay, the boy I become is
the boy who holds space in my dreams

bought, not   *bothered*
with knowing how to explain himself or
apologizing for things he cannot control

cool, calm,   *collected*

the ideal rent this boy – at times
his bones ache from the pressure

that is transforming people, while   *transformed*

he remembers this body is medicine, curing
confused white men who think I need them

more than they   *need me.*
how do you distinguish love from sex?

he asks, I   *tell him*
sex fills me up & love reminds me
it's okay to be empty

meet me by mars

meet me by mars?

"$100 to suck you off"

meet me by mars?

"if you're hot, sex work comes to you in concrete metropolitan cities"

meet me by mars?

the request is that I get naked immediately after the door locks

meet me by mars?

don't comment on the apartment or the view

meet me by mars?

i say cash up front—he says dick first

where the fuck is mars?

if I had known he lived in the penthouse maybe i'd have asked for more

GREGORY SCOFIELD

the dancer (club mix)

see him   he is
un touchable, unreadable,

more lovely than smooth gravity
glistening

down the length of his body
his small hips, his tight

perfect ass swinging
up to the platform, all motion

swivelling on his golden ball-bearings.
see him   moving

on rhythmic cue, he is
beautiful, so unreadable

the curve of his spine
is the jigsaw puzzle

we want to put together,
the damp lush scene   he is

getting paid
to unlock his vaulted package,

the overflowing box
of our stone-dragging youth.

but   we are falling
at his feet, longing

to take each biblical toe
into our mouths, praying

to be his stigmata, oh
his incubus-tongued angel,

love eye-d, all sugar-eyed
like the e-queens bopping high,

messed on their own love trip tripping
though we're all chasing

locks, zippers,
the elastic band

holding his jockstrap together.
but   he is

getting paid a doctor's wage
to be that fat man's murderer,

the old troll's executioner, a killer
made more lovely

stroking the blade of his
oh so deadly nipples.

and beneath the red light
he will be the boy in school

who beat the shit out of us
for looking: he will be

our velvet fuck, our burly-man prince,
our mint-

flavoured lamb, our saviour ... but see
he is   grazing down his belly,

all ten fingers
an arsenal to keep us smouldering.

we can smell
the gunpowder between his legs

and we want to pop, pop
pop

because he is getting paid
to fuck our minds, getting paid

to make us forget our mirrors,
the crystal-dropping twinks

floating to the dance floor,
bouncing like muppets.

because   he is
getting paid

to make the drag queens feel
like real women, getting paid

to be their spank-spank boy,
the roughneck quarterback

running them past the goal line
of snickering small towns,

fathers who just wouldn't understand,
but see   he is

all muscle, his perfect ass swinging.
he is our golden trumpet,

our rainbow flat anthem:
Everybody wants to be somebody

Everybody wants to be somebody
Everybody wants to be somebody

Everybody wants to be somebody

and he is   getting paid
by the man upstairs who
discovered his ass,
knew it

would be a money-maker, a ching-
ching factory of coke-den lies,

a bar tab of heart
heart

heartbreak – but see   he is
un touchable, unreadable,

more lovely than smooth gravity
glistening, sliding

down the length of his
          bones.

but he is getting paid
at the end of the night and

these are some of the bones
he takes home; his

mother's narrow foot
dancing away from him, his

grandmother's hairpins
falling into a drawer

deep in his memory, the blood
bursting inside his aunty's head

while she was sleeping,
drunk ... and his own

aching bones,
half-breed and kicking.

yet later, swallowed by
the empty mouths of our beds,

we will think of him.
we will make him pay.

he will be our second-hand   doll
and we will use him

for free, as if
he meant nothing

Lost Fingers

I am sucking for fortunes in an old whore's bodice
I am kanada—
lost fingers,
lost in amerika's underwear.
Get a touch of poetry from a poet/cactus
my opera lover fills the orifice
of the frog king.
They have nothing, I have everything,
find me some fingers
I'll eat 'em,
they'll be building another temple yet
on the hill where I was born.
It's all in the nose and the wise wicked mouths,
lost fingers in the ocean.
I am the sea, lost fingers in me.
Bring it back slowly.
Your poets need you—
your nails scratch and murder
stay   stay   stay
muscle fizzle
I don't need you that bad.

LESTER MAYERS

Cynicism

> "Because rape on the body of a young person more often than
> not introduces cynicism, and there is nothing quite so tragic
> as a young cynic, because it means the person has gone from
> knowing nothing to believing nothing."
> —Maya Angelou

The rescue of the morning sun gazed upon his bruised,
bloody black body kicking awake his reality.
The sounds of the semi-busy Brooklyn street tore through
the 2014 Aéropostale hoodie that covered his ears.
The screeching buses which could've easily been confused
with screams of terror at midnight ... stopped to let off faces
of plum, yellow, honey human beings whose voices mixed perfectly
with beeping horns and loud cellphone talkers whose conversations
probably were heard a block away.

Children's morning grunts and elders' "Good morning" prayer
was thrust upon strangers they passed on the street.
It was another day for him.

Another survived attack of selling his body to dick gone wrong.
Just hours earlier he trolled the back ends of Harlem looking for a John
who choked and punched him dead in the eye after he requested his pay
from a job well done.

After the brutal attack at the hands of a "married straight man"
he hopped on the downtown C train on 116 Street leaking blood
at 2:30 in the morning. The hunger pains in his stomach and the fearful tremor
that controlled his breath began to dissipate as he began making his way toward
Brooklyn. A place where he knew no one would inquire about his face/well-being
and plights. He would be invisible.
To him invisibility meant safety.

Yawning and stretching through last night's disappointments
and confusions of morning cultural-madness, he found the strength
and quick intelligence
that the street taught him to grab his backpack
that had been tucked between his legs ·
and rush to the nearest Clean Rite Laundromat.

When he arrived, the owners were in the back cleaning out dryers
and whipping down washing machines from the night before.
He snuck into the restroom and began to make his morning ablutions.
He reached into his backpack and pulled out a three-toned stained towel
that had gone from white to brown and roughly rubbed the hard dried blood
that covered his face like snot on a 2-year-old child on a winter's day.
He pulled out a wrinkled pair of brown pants and a purple collared shirt
with a school logo on it to costume his ashy body.
He sneakily exited the laundromat and treaded
toward school to make it in time for breakfast.
"Good morning, Ms Johnson."
Ms Johnson grunted at him, hinting at the usual disappointment
of his wrinkled uniform and disheveled, untended to skin and hair.
"Good morning, Ujasiri, tuck in that shirt and put some lotion on."

Ujasiri laughed to himself.

Ms Johnson was the closest thing to a mother he had.

She was a blunt, lightly toasted buttered black woman with short hair and glasses.

She could hear a fly landing against a wall in a room full of loud of teenagers.

She spoke with the diction of God and had the arms of a noble black woman

who could "Throw zown in the kitchen."

The students hated her ass; she was the law.

She treated everyone with the same respect and held everyone

to the same standards no matter how they presented themselves.

She was the dean of students but in true black woman fashion

she quadrupled as a: cook, therapist, pastor and sometimes doctor.

Parents knew when she called home, she meant business.

The clock flew like tears on the face of a motherless child

that just received news of their morning turned mourning.

School was out and the biggest task of staying low-key was achieved.

The afternoon warmth settled on the concrete ground

creating a fragrance of spring.

A fragrance that greeted the energized children

that now flooded the temporarily abandoned streets.

Children ran home, or to after-school programs,

while Ujasiri headed to the library where he routinely did his homework

and read up on ideas from the greatest minds of literature like:

Maya Angelou, James Baldwin, Edna St Vincent Millay and Tennessee Williams.

He always had hope that he would be as great as them.

With inspiration running through his mind,

spinning down to his finger tips and dripping out his pen,

with unmitigated gall he writes:

"THE GRACE OF MORNING ALIGNED HIS FACE
THE PULSE OF EVENING FORMED HIS SMILES
THE PEAK OF MIDNIGHT COLOURED HIS EYES
THE INSTINCTS OF SURVIVAL SCRAPED HIS KNEES
THE PAINS OF LIFE SCARRED HIS WRIST
THE THOUGHTS OF DEATH INTRUDED HIS MIND
THE FEAR OF LOVE STRUCTURED HIS SPINE
THE RESCUE OF THE MORNING SUN GAZED UPON HIS BRUISED,
BLOODY BLACK SKIN KICKING AWAKE HIS COURAGE
TO BREATHE AGAIN."

NAOMI SAYERS

A Memory I Need to Talk About

I get bogged down with other thoughts on my mind. These thoughts take up the majority of my waking hours and I don't know why I think about them constantly. I have been thinking about this one memory since my dad has passed. I used to strip in my hometown of Sault Ste. Marie, Ontario. I had people come up to me to tell me that they heard from their grandmother. "Well, I didn't see your grandma at the club," I would tell them, and then I would laugh it off. Home was about twenty minutes outside of the city limits. It was a First Nations, so no cab company would pick up rides from the First Nations going into the city and they wouldn't take rides back to the First Nations either.

I have hitchhiked before.
My father knew that I would do it again.

The first time I hitchhiked, it was dark, cold, and it might have been raining. I remember my parents came to look for me, but I hid in the ditch. I didn't want to be found. When I was younger, I put my parents through a lot. But that night my dad drove me to work, and I think about this a lot, I think about how much he loved me. I don't remember what we talked about or if we even talked at all. I remember him driving up to the club and I remember telling him thank you for the ride, Dad. Like always, I remember saying, "See you love you."

And, you see, that is the thing about sex work in the north,
especially if you are an Indigenous woman.
There is a lot of unsafe ways to do it.

And sometimes those ways put Indigenous women at risk of going missing or murdered. But, also, there are safer ways to engage in sex work and sometimes that means relying on family for rides. And then there's these dangerous narratives, and the laws supporting those narratives, that presume that an Indigenous woman, especially a young Indigenous woman, is being trafficked and is being trafficked by her family. If my dad had not driven me that night, I know that I would have opted for a more unsafe way to get to work. Who knows if I would have even made it work. And I have been thinking about this car ride.

I want to sit in the car with him one more time
and to tell him thank you for keeping me safe.

What Stigmatizes You Makes You Stronger

Released
JANUARY
10 months of the system
1 month being homeless

A girlfriend from the shelter
and I get an apartment of our own
Roommates in a safe place, we promise
each other, a safe place

A social worker drops
off my life in garbage bags

My life:
rejected victim service letters
university books and papers
our drums
Post-it note poems

But not even a month later
my roommate's scary date
(the scariest white guy)
She's too gone to realize
that we're not safe

My mind obsessed by horrible headlines
What if we're busted and blamed
or what if he attacks
kidnaps us
kills us

I hide out on the reserve
slightly safer

I still make my university classes
I still get sent to student union conferences

But there's only so much
protection on the rez

Blonde police officer drives me
back to my apartment from the rez
She thinks my problems are the rez
oblivious to the real danger

Can't remember which class I have tomorrow
It's time to make a plan

What stigmatizes you (could kill you) makes you stronger, right?
I speak up
I reach out

I call a sex worker organization
the frontline angel on the phone
"you're the expert of your experience."
I tell her "I need help with my safety"

I tell some of the men on the rez
and they listen
they get ready

Alright scary midlife white man
who talks about cutting up women in my home
who likes to put his hands on me
Listen. You're in my fucking world, pal
My roommate is 21 years old
and not sure if she'll see 22

I wish you luck on this one
You'll need it

Strong native men know who you are
they will protect the home
of two native women

This is NOT the story of how
I let some motherfucker take over my life

This is the story of how I spoke up
of how I called upon my resources
worked two jobs just to thrive
This is a story of how I survived

Can't Be Discovered

Living every 21-year-old girl's dream
by celebrating my birthday
in a homeless shelter

Also my scene: University
My campus look: half updos
H&M black knee-high socks
Makeup tactics

Dress like other female students
Besides, homeless chic look is in
except I really am a street bitch

Can't be discovered
Can't let my worlds collide

I go to welfare office visits between classes
I meet my social worker at the campus caf

after biology lab I take the bus
to the drop-in women's center to eat

I show my Foucault books
to the other girls at the shelter

Look out old school institution
we might just take over

Can't be discovered
Can't let my worlds collide

When I Crossed the Border

Poem for three overlapping voices bringing together various experiences of underground migration.

When I crossed the border
I knew no one and had nothing

    When I crossed the border
    I still had little boxes of sweets from the bakery in my hometown

        When I crossed the border
        I had a SIM card with credit and 400 dollars

When I crossed the border they asked me question after question
Like a criminal, like an alien, subhuman

    When I crossed the border I hid in a meatpacking
    Truck taking tiny little breaths

        When I crossed the border I didn't know
        What work I would do and where
        When I crossed the border I paid a mafia to smuggle me in

Took on a debt, $30,000 to pay off over a year or two or five
Because there was no legal way to get in, there was no dignified way

When I crossed the border I turned off my christianity
To make money for a house I could come back to and pray

I didn't want to stay in Italy—there's no money

I didn't want to stay in France—they're all racist

I wanted to work in Birmingham, there's work in Birmingham,
and family

When I crossed the border I was arrested
I was sent to Yarl's Wood detention centre
For weeks, months, a year with no news

When I crossed the border I felt sick, clandestine
Carrying a constant tension, fear that someone will find me out

When I braved the border I did it for my family

No papers, no safety, no bank account, no work

I did it to escape war

When I crossed the border they said "no" ...

To escape occupation

No papers, no safety, no bank account, no work

They deported me once, twice, again, again

        No papers, no safety, no bank account, no work

    To escape corruption

When I crossed the border I did things I didn't want to do
Things I had to do, to build a better life, to live at all

    To escape a destroyed economy

        No papers, no safety, no bank account, no work

When I crossed the border I was tired of the wages in my country barely buying bread

    Never recovered from colonialism

        No papers, no safety, no bank account, no work

I got here and the people were cold and the life expensive

    No, colonized still!

        No papers, no safety, no bank account, no work

But the currency so strong that I could buy 10 times more at home

    When I crossed the border I crossed my own borders

        No papers, no safety, no bank account, no work

When I crossed the border I did it for my family

Low pay shit jobs treated like nothing despite my degree

No papers, no safety, no bank account, no work

When I crossed the border
[together] I had to make a new me

You especially,

This is not a poem about migration, the validity of the horizon line, the questions
asked at security checkpoints, how Korean women who cross borders have
always been treated with suspicion, the last time you were denied at customs.
This is not a poem about the certainty found in maps and atlases, the formations
made in the sky by our own invisible flight patterns, the way geese stop to wait
for each other, how the north star is always found on the way to mecca.
This is not a poem about the mistletoe, how it slowly takes over a white oak, and
does not let up, the way the yellow swallowtail is imprinted
to cross great distances.

This is not a poem about having lost something, turning the world over with
regret, wishing I had stopped to say how much you mean to me.
This is not a poem about echolocation, the sonar that dolphins and whales use
to find each other, the way their calls permeate the density of water and how the
honey bee
can still communicate despite smoke and everyday obstacles.

This is a poem is about me and you,
and you especially who I have not yet met.
The sisterhood behind closed doors, beneath mood lighting,
how your work is miscalculated,
the quiet eruption of underground volcanoes,
the way we were never meant to be seen.

This is a poem about how my own two hands could never forget the labor
of my body   or yours.
This is a poem about reaching past a locked gate, a secured fence, our own
closed hearts, and knowing, we cannot stop the songs of migratory birds,
or keep a monarch caterpillar from reaching for the milkweed,
we cannot wrestle bones away from wolves,
or stop the earth from being eclipsed.

JAENE F. CASTRILLON

A Celebration of Darkness

"A certain darkness is needed to see the stars."
—Osho

1. The Field

Open field surrounded by trees, wind BLOWING, grass
swaying, leaves RUSTLING in the WIND. FOOTSTEPS IN GRASS.
ADULT JANE, Indigenous female 39 with scars on her arm, explores the field.
MOTHER GODDESS, 65 female, appears.
MOTHER GODDESS: You are a divine manifestation of the beloved. Your presence
and being is worthy of love. You are a beautiful, unique and loved organism
within the cosmos.
Adult Jane hand plays with a CLEAR QUARTZ CRYSTAL. Raises crystal to
sun.
Crystal glinting from sun. Eyes reflecting glints. She squints.

2. The Child's Bedroom
MOTHER GODDESS: You have survived your trial by fire and now you are ready
to behold your destiny.

MUFFLED YELLING
THINGS BEING KNOCKED DOWN
FOOTSTEPS TO ROOM

CHILD JANE, Indigenous female 12, blinking. Her POV of the bedroom door. BLANKET pulled up to eyes. Dark room. Shadows. Door is creaks open. Child Jane BREATHING.

Blanket pulled overhead. Room has STUFFED TOYS, BEAR STUFF, CRYSTALS, SMALL TABLE FAN, PERSONALIZED MIRROR, MOON NIGHT LIGHT, CURTAINS SWAY in the WIND. Shadow monster creeping across the room. Child Jane under the blankets, squeezing her eyes tightly closed. CREEPY HAND looms across wall, shadow travels across blanket. CREEPY HAND grabs blanket. Fan BLOWS, curtain GENTLY FLAPS, blanket NOISES. Tree SHADOW on wall. Breathing, fan blowing, curtain flapping, blanket noises reaches a CRESCENDO. Everything is COMPLETELY SILENT.

MOTHER GODDESS: These crystals are connected to the sacred divine; through them you are unbroken, unsullied and whole. You have purpose and destiny; these crystals are your gifts.

CREEPY HAND creeps to closet door. Child Jane wrapped in blanket, sits on the floor, only her face is showing. Moon night light shines, crystal reflections play on the wall mixed with shadows of trees.

MOTHER GODDESS: You believe humanity's will to triumph, no matter the darkness.
You believe in the stupor of love, to fall wholeheartedly, fragile and broken
You believe you will persevere no matter the challenge.

Lush Trees, WIND RUSTLING LEAVES. Moving through grass. Landing on Adult Jane's back. Adult Jane's face mixed with crystal lights and glare. Sitting in a field, Adult Jane knits a CROWN OF FLOWERS. FLOWERS at her feet. Adult Jane and Child Jane intermix. Crystal reflections take over. Child Jane falls face up back into bed.

3. Addiction

BLOOD swirls in WATER. Blood drops on a RAZOR BLADE. HAMMER smashes MIRROR TO PIECES. Blood on broken mirror. A time lapse ROTTING STRAWBERRY.

BLACK BLOOD takes over water. BLACK blood drowns the razor. Struggling in RESTRAINTS. PILL taking. Looking at mirror. Reflections of laughing, crying, frantic rambling, threatening, scratching, pulling hair. Suddenly stoic and sullen. RED NAIL POLISH. SHINY RED lips and smoking. Lots of headlights and TRAFFIC. COUNTING MONEY, OPEN a CONDOM. Lipstick re-application. Pouring ALCOHOL, POT, COCAINE and ECSTACY PILLS on glass. FROST FLOWER BLOOM   ICE SUNSET   STORM projected on a BEDSHEET. Wrapped up like Child Jane.

MOTHER GODDESS: You believe that life is meant to be beautiful. You believe in
having a purpose, in being an embodiment of love. You believe. You believe?

4. Flowers

Adult Jane HUMMING. Hands make a crown of flowers. Reflections and light. Adult Jane blinks. CRYING, THUMPING, HEAVY BREATHING, CREAKING DOOR. Crystal reflections play on skin, on face, on scars.

MOTHER GODDESS: Is there beauty in madness? Is the madness a symptom of a
sick world or is the madness a sign that you are seeing unfettered by the chains of
illusion. Blossoming like a field of flowers, you can feel their petals gently caress
you. Maybe the voices are really just the wind whispering LOVE.
ECHO.

Adult Jane looks at the sky. Shields her eyes. A COPPER BOWL of water. CRYSTAL being washed. SMUDGE SHELL smoking with SAGE. Crystals smoke with smudge. TOBACCO TIES on a string. HUMMING. SONG.

5. The Prayer

Eyes peer through leaves. CREATURE JANE is fierce and feral. Tobacco tied loosely looped around neck. Eyes are glittery and dark. Lips red and moist. She is in the FOREST.

Creature Jane comes upon a clearing. She lights a BONFIRE. The WOOD BURNS BRIGHT. Creature Jane holds the crystal, firelight reflected on it. She puts SMUDGE and PALO SANTO to the fire. SMOKE floats to the sky. MUMBLING in a trance. There are BONES, ROCKS AND BOWLS around the FIREPIT. Smoke rises. Her face reflects the flames. Her eyes glowing. Creature Jane puts on a BEAR SKIN. She places HEADPIECE on her head. Eyes closed. BREATHES DEEPLY. She smears blue paint across her eyes, then puts on a CROWN OF BEAR CLAWS and TEETH. Her eyes open suddenly.

Creature Jane writhes in possession. She throws tobacco into the fire. She gestures at the FIRE, to the sky. She turns toward the sky and roars, smoke coming out of her mouth. STORM CLOUDS, SUNRISING, STARS on a draped bedsheet.

6. Bear Warrior

MOTHER GODDESS: In this moment you are so taken by beauty that you toss
   your wildflower infused hair back to laugh loudly. You are whirling around with
   your arms outstretched to the sky above, as the landscape swirls around you. You
   laugh and swirl. You are the vibrancy of colours, smell and sigh. What is the light
   without darkness? What is life without living?

Creature Jane's forest travels intermingle with Adult Jane whirling in the field.
Dizzy Adult Jane falls faceup in a field. Child Jane simultaneously falls from
darkness to land in the same field side by side with Adult Jane. Adult Jane turns
to face Child Jane. Adult Jane reaches out to grasp Child Jane's hand. They mir-
ror each other. Adult Jane smiles at Child Jane. Adult Jane touches Child Jane's
sad face. Adult Jane mouths the words "I love you" to Child Jane. They smile to
each other. Child Jane FADES AWAY.
Adult Jane holds Child Jane's hand till Child Jane fades away. ADULT JANE
smiles and opens her hand to reveal a DARK QUARTZ CRYSTAL.

MOTHER GODDESS: You are utterly in love. What is the distinction between you
   and this swirling world?

Adult Jane lifts dark crystal to sun. Not squinting. Rainbow crystal refracts
over her arms, face and hair. Adult Jane hugs dark crystal to chest, eyes closed,
smiling. Lying facedown on the ground, Adult Jane puts dark crystal an arm's
length away. She crosses her arms to admire it in the sun.

DANCING REFLECTIONS, REFRACTIONS, RAINBOWS of CRYSTAL and
LIGHTS. BREATHING.

STICKIE STACKEDHOUSE

to my clients who tell me i look tired

i am

because your dick is the 8th one today

And bitch there's always more

because the scent i obscure myself in reminds me of lost cousins

because queer community doesn't hold me

because, on tinder, fem4fem is a myth or a hat some people wear sometimes

because my community is full of secret liberals whose ears are closed to my class, to my anger

because self care is about isolation

because for the millionth time bbbj is not on today's menu

because, for now, I have two friends with civvie jobs that will lend me money

and that's better to any dad dick

because i still can't afford a new magic wand?!?

because you can only thrive on ramen noodles for so long

because the neighbours call the city on our house of made-up family

because the cops follow me and harass me for wearing garter belts

because i just want someone to fuck me right (or is that a performance?)

because i can't turn all straight and find a rich man

because masculinity has always bored me

because her lips are sweet and unattainable

because the bees are dying and i can't make my rent

because im scared of the living potential of being a trope

because i still believe in love touch or loving touch

because somewhere under here and all of this i could find it in me to eat you surely,

split you from tip to tip and ask you, "honey, what's your real name?"

CASSANDRA BLANCHARD

XXX

I must have turned a thousand tricks over those six years, you name it I've done it, the perfect whore, young-looking so the men buzzed around me like bees on honey, you have no idea how many men see working girls for a quick blow job in the car after work before going home or taxi drivers or stockbrokers, all kinds like the author of children's books or the man who was a politician in Native self-government or probably your boyfriend or husband, there are the real cold mean ones and the okay ones who were not that bad and I mostly had middle-aged married white men and I guarantee that you know someone who has paid for sex; once I did a blow job where he blew his load in exactly three seconds or the vampire-looking dude with a foot-long boner that made me almost piss myself, but it's always been strictly business, I've been around the block for sure. At a Quebecois rehab centre, there was the gender rule, *no breaking gender*, as in no fucking with either gender and of course I broke that rule multiple times, at night when everyone was asleep I would slide into bed with my woman and quietly make her cum, I couldn't not do it and it didn't help when a chick would get a crush on me, I guess I had to break the rules, it felt so good to be bad—I've never even been on a date before, it has always been straight to screwing, I guess it would be nice to go out for dinner rather than sleeping with someone in secret, for two years we were together, the violent psycho and me, the pushover, but damn we clicked in the sack and everywhere too, like in a semi or on the bus or outside, the only time we got along was when we were fucking, this bitch was a sociopath, I swear her eyes had nothing behind them, but even though I was in danger around her, she made me feel safe and made me feel like I was losing the hamster wheel race, seriously though, I've had enough to last me three thousand years and that's nothing to be happy about, being for sale ain't nothing to be proud of.

Love I

I thought it was love but really it was exploitation, it took me years to comprehend how much Kayla had damaged me and my soul and my sanity and especially my trust of other people—relationships that are based on drugs are never healthy, it's like a rotten peach, it looks good on the outside but once you bite it, it's all rotten on the inside; I went from being a partner to a cash cow to feed our drug habits and our desperation and rootlessness haunted us until there was no respect anymore, like a lone shoestring, the only thing that held us together was sex whether it was us making love or for men who paid me a lot of money for services—I remember the first time I ever turned a trick, I was nineteen and when a dealer asked for a blow job I said that I didn't do that kind of stuff and of course behind my back he asks Kayla if I would do it for a substantial amount of crack, she didn't ask me she told me and therefore I did it and that started an influx of dates. Once these exchanges began to be normal for us, the respect she had for me vanished and I was no longer a person but a means to get more money and drugs, violence came with it and it came slowly until she was head-butting me on the street or pulling my hair or scaring me with a hunting knife and I had to deal with her psychosis, which was unbearable; I am sure Kayla is cold inside, but she did make me feel warm and I loved her though I had every reason not to and I wonder now if she's dead or alive and if she is alive what her life is like and then I get angry because why should I care.

Maple Ridge

Somehow we ended up in Maple Ridge where we stayed for week or so at this dude's place and then went out for days hunting money for drugs while Kim got almost-daily western-union money from her sugar daddy, our combined drug habits needed more cash so I did what she trained me to do and that was servicing men for money and I remember hustling on this block called North Road late at night and this one guy who I had a date with never picked up a girl before so he was nervous and generous with money, I could state any price and I have to admit I felt sorry for the bloke, he looked like he was going to piss himself, this block on North Road was dark and dangerous and the business was pretty good, I didn't think too much about danger cuz if I did I would not be able to do this shit and if I was not able to do this shit then I would be punished and pressured to get back into it and it was guaranteed money, which was the most important thing, it was like drugs were more important than my life, so this one dude picked me up and I actually preferred his company over Kayla's and so I spent time with him, he was an okay guy but cuz of my misplaced sense of loyalty I called Kayla in front of him and he told me I sounded like I was afraid of her and he didn't want to become part of it so I left and went back doing the same old bullshit; there was a crack house in Maple Ridge we frequented for a bit run by a scary dude named Dodd who was pretty decent to me and I met this woman there who hustled as well and she was disturbed by how young I was and that I was doing this shit and other people were often disturbed that Kayla, who supposedly loved me, would let me do something like sell myself to help feed our expensive habits, but in the end everything is all about money.

Lonely Men

There are these men who are so lonely they feel the need to make friends when all you want is a quick and easy business deal, these men are so pathetic that I feel sorry for them as they hold my hand and talk about their day or try to kiss or cuddle imagining I'm their wife or something, however fulfilling fantasies was what I did for drug money so I held their hands while they drove around and engaged in affectionate conversation and smoked the cigarettes they gave me and ate the food they offered me; with these kind of guys, getting tips is practically guaranteed and even better was getting them to become a regular as it's easy money and I only had to accept the affection they gave, which was strangely harder to do than it being strictly business, these men are pretty vanilla and aren't into pain or humiliation and are all in all pretty decent, however there are always exceptions; there are men who managed to make me feel like a nasty crack whore, leaving bruises all over my body or grabbing my hair telling me to take it down the throat and I'd better swallow what they gave cuz they're paying good money and this goes on and on and soon they become a blur of faces; the only way I could stand it was the thought of smoking a big rock and to keep smoking it until everything faded away.

I made it

I made it through the icy cold.
I made it through the thistle.
I made it through the raging fires of racism and discrimination.
I made it through hurricanes of heartache and through a vortex of loss.
I made it through the paths of hell to face my mental torment.
I made it, standing tall, on my back and crawling on my knees for forgiveness.
I made it supported with the greatest love
and I made it alone.

I made it despite the fact that the world said I shouldn't have.
And since, I made it then, and made it through the times when I was stripped
of all of my powers, not recognizing the eyes that looked back on me from the
mirror and I truly lost all hope.
I'm pretty sure I'll make it now.

de.vour

/dɪˈvaʊɚ/

1. I wanted to be ruined more than I wanted to be loved, pain is more intense than pleasure and my body is a weapon I don't know how to love gently with.
2. We are self sufficient in our suffering, know how to use this to our advantage, know how to work a crowd.
3. Dress up just to dress down, all lace and skin and skin.
4. Who is the victim here?

HALF ASSED ATTEMPTS AT TALKING ABOUT IT

1. God turned his back on me long before I turned mine on Him, you were twelve years old in His house with your body being laid out on a table for the vultures, screaming *Father, why have you forsaken me.*

2. Deleted poetry, there is nothing to see here, no evidence. There are no photos spanning the years I was sick because I convinced myself I wouldn't fit in the frame.

3. I say, "I think I might've been abused" and she looks at me and says, "No shit, what was your first clue?"

4. Tired of fucking to feel whole, reptilian girl using their bodies as a heat source, see the scales of her skin where it flakes off? I don't know if I feel human anymore.

5. The bathroom tiles are stained red and my bed has become a crime scene, I wake up still tasting nightmares. My room is a self-inflicted jail cell I am unable to leave.

6. It is 1 a.m. and I am being carried to the backseat of the car screaming, there is blood on my face and bugs under my skin and I make eye contact with my little sister through the window as we pull out of the driveway.

7. I am so sorry, this isn't your fault, I was soaked in sin at birth and it's so hard to scrub clean.

8. This time I'm in the front seat, his hands are on my waist. Pretty little jailbait, you have eyes like a rabbit and it's time to run run run and don't look back.

9. White walls white halls, strip lighting and starched uniforms. A tube leaks life back into my veins and I want to say "you are a doctor not a necromancer, you can't bring back what's already dead."

10. I am sorry for forcing you to sit back and watch me self-destruct.

MOON DANCER

Her/Us

endanger her

enable us/endanger us/

main purpose

major plus/enable us/

same purpose

ponderous/male versus

same service

HYSTERIKA

Going to Hell

"Most likely I will go to hell and most likely I deserve to be there."
—from *The House on Mango Street* by Sandra Cisneros

"Shame on you!" is the sound of my mother's voice inside my head
"God damn you all to hell!" she would say
Oh, and my personal favourite
"You think you can just do whatever you jolly well please."
These are the words permanently emblazoned on my brain
Whenever I think of my mother
And if there is a price to be paid for playfulness
in the Afterlife
Then surely I will be indebted for all of eternity
For few have shirked the shawl of seriousness
With the bound determination that I have
Indeed, I have danced upon the grave
Of all that is truly and honourably grave.
And I have done it in clear plexi platform stilettos
The kind with the shiny silver straps
And I have done it naked as the day I was born
Circling my hot pink lace bra overhead
And slingshotting it into the crowd while I'm
Twerking for Jesus
And his hair is metaphorically tied back in a gorgeous yoga man bun
And he's wearing Mardi Gras beads and a candy necklace
And one of those big Number 1 foam hands

And in this metaphor we look
Like Miley Cyrus and Robin Thicke
And it's not going to get more dignified than this
Because someday when I get to Heaven
We will go backstage
And I will lift his golden white robes
And give him a sweet down 'n' dirty blowy
For a crisp brown hundie
And while I am down there
On my knees anyway
I will hear the voice of my mother
Inside my head
And I will offer up this prayer:
Oh father, forgive me
For I have rimmed
the edge of my glass
with sugar.

Gospel

Here is some bad poetry written by a good hooker.
Now present your hand and I'll sit on your face.

The only thing I've ever sold is patience,
and yet They still investigate.

There isn't much that makes me
squirm. I've seen their insides,

all the pink and all the shit
and still they ask for no rubber.

They live off my maternal burden
as some of us spread our thighs,

legs facing up to the sky
other spread lies.

Try to guess who comes out as the Devil in this charade.
They cry *pandered children* but they never once open the door.

They even built arenas to watch us,
like gladiators covered in baby oil and mascara.

But as the end days come near
They worry about their legacy

as it must be preserved.
Ironically, there will be no one left.

So the real trick here is to try not to see.
Use the shutters and turn up the TV.

Noon prayers on rug-burned knees

The last time I made salat
was under a waning crescent moon
mouth mumbling forgotten prayers

up, down, up—
prostrating
on knees
in front of God

instead of a customer
forever grateful that
my Creator
refused to be called (Father
I cut off
limb rotting in Midwest cornfields)
a trinity of "Daddy issues"

Catholic guilt
sperm donor
and the Holy Spirit of sucking cock

avoided
by demanding more.

Sheikh says
memorizing 99 names
will let me enter paradise

dissociation speaks louder
a buzzing noise in my ear.
I forget my own most days.

Jagged gaps in my mind
and I still hold on   maybe

one day I will (not) forget You.

this is not mythology

drowned pickled men
I pick this treasure floating out of their bloated pockets and into my palm
not whores we are
The Nereides
but you may also say Goddess

siren   cackling with friends, pillow
             case fights on slick rocks, sweetly licking salt
             off lips, kissing savory tongues

I relish this brine
call me slick
mermaid girl
$300 will get you wet when
            I soak myself
            skip the flush
            leave you sopping and slip
            out rich

shore, we learned to walk on
land,
but it's just for show

sure, some
times my shins splint
splayed

cracked and
dry from   fric
                 tion

still,
walk till day's cashed
then stride back
slide through the silky   skin   of ocean
                                                    salt and supple muscles
                                                    like wow

in chorus, girls:
suck the sea like a fetish
and spit!

terra firma, drenched!
spit!
man splatter, puffed! and shattered!

then
ocean fall, back
to liquid seabed
and   rest.

                    hey, mermaid girl
                       with that
                    wet slip shining
                       siren slide
                     of every girl
               with a $300 stride to dock

sleepytime tea

chamomile and blackcurrant tea
gone cold-curdled.
filter it like ash through your teeth.

2:22 a.m. and today is a day of
budgeting. can you afford the specialist
even with insurance can you sleepwalk
crooked-charm teeth bared through
medication appeals your whole
body hurts. and you have one
loyal john and he's gone cold.

it tasted like freedom, drowsy-steeped
after your first paycheck. you kept your
ad up "just in case" but the house spider
in your rotting windows had
an egg sac and complacent with
spring's promise they all hatched at once.

charlotte's web ends with the spider
dying because she's not as
important as the pig.

your straight job means you have folders
upon folders you struggle with. envelopes

untidy lingerie tucked sorted away.
the tax department sends you another caution.
another power bill. another blood test.

your wife files job application after application.
"let me know," that one john texts and:
calendar emergency -ologist appointments
working every weekend for months
"get in touch in a week or two, when
hopefully things will have settled down"

contour your body's warning signs into
fever-dreams of nymphomaniac overstimulation.
therapist long-discarded suggested
it might not be good to keep working, not
like this. you think about how
many bookings it took to see her.

how long have you been explaining the
freezer burn consuming your limbs away as
coming so hard you can't walk afterward?
"take it as a compliment." twin laughs.

you give him meeting points closer and
closer to your house as walking grows hard.
step into his car and let him let you
pretend you don't need this. let you let
him pretend you do want him.

put the kettle on when you get home,
won't you? you'll need it.

beatitudes

dear mom and dad,

blessed are the poor in spirit,

if the government finds out i talk to you two at all
they'll have me charged with welfare fraud.

blessed are the peacemakers,

"dad was—" the gay auckland business association interviewer told me not to
continue. assumed that you raped me. looked at the way i flinched and gave me a
scholarship that didn't exist before their pity did.
"and then mom—" the studylink interviewer cut in, voice soft and shallow-sweet.
you can't go home, can you, she asked, and no, i said, no, i can't,
crossed my nerve-damaged fingers behind my back.

blessed are those who hunger for righteousness,

you would have me back any day if i were willing, or desperate,
but not me.
smooth your housework-calloused fingers across my brow
lay your big warm hand on my head
and pray for your baby girl to recover.
turn back to god.
like faith would heal all the things i was born and all the things i became.

blessed are the meek,

like your baby girl didn't die in that late-term abortion,
dad praying a million prayers outside the operating room
where they cut mom open and told him
you have to choose one,
we can't save both mother and fetus,
and they put me in an incubator and told you both that
they'd done the impossible.
your baby girl
is a miracle. they said. and you believed it.

    blessed are those who mourn,

here is the truth:

your daughter died the moment the doctors removed my
viscera-coated unmoving body like a tumour from your abdomen
looked at my genitals and hesitated.

    blessed are the pure of heart,

congenital adrenal hyperplasia feels sticky in your mouth like the
life-support cocktail of corticosteroids your daughter
took as a syrup. she was four years old and she
thought it was for her lungs
because she was born so early and it's only half true.

    blessed are the persecuted,

when your daughter was nine years old they operated on her.
her surgeons were only half a decade older at most undressing her on the
makeshift operating table of a school bus floor and they say
you're not normal and we need to fix it
draw their surgeon's tools from unzipped pencil cases and unzipped pants
and tell her to hold still.
she has been touched by too many doctors already to think
that she doesn't need to obey.

   blessed are the merciful,

a decade later she is a corpse. handcuffed to my throat as i run
away from home
and you search for her instead.
i am newly nineteen and i have no idea that she is rotting inside me,
homeless and no health insurance and no birth certificate and no reason why
my body is falling apart cortisol so low my testosterone burns through
me like my nightmares
and bones that x-rays say are ten years older than my body is
and she is dead.

   blessed are those who are persecuted

i hide behind her name for two more years.
file papers for a name change and think about my
conspiracy theorist flatmate who says that
really, a birth certificate is a death certificate.

   for the sake of righteousness,

i never work up the courage to break the news to you.
even now you message me and the name you call is hers,
i message you about my faltering body and the truths
it carries that i have finally discovered.
you tell me that i am sick. and you tell me to come home
so you can
lay your hands on your daughter's decomposing corpse
and pray.

for theirs is the kingdom of heaven.

dear mom and dad,

i am sorry to tell you that your daughter died
slowly and painfully.

JASBINA JUSTICE

Witch, always.

I was always the witch. This is a word in a tongue that is not mine but will do.
I am terror when you make me the other, but if you stand with me I become
    possibility.
Find me in the woods, sharpening my axe, sewing my bags, and waiting.
Smell the blood. Lick the earth, and listen for my laugh.

Slippery, sticky, messy, gooey.

Rich running over hands.
Massaged into thirsty hair.
Dry skin.   Curving hips.
Full breasts released   from black lace bras
Heavy and pulled down   by gravity's hands.
        Grease it all.
            Moisturize.
                Moist. Wet.
                    Pampered.
Lavender oil and shea butter   everywhere.
Every part oiled   lovingly.
A black bush parted   revealing folds
blushing deeper rose with each touch.
        Marvel and stretch.
Luxuriating in so much perfect skin   and sinew.
            Muscle and mass.
Releasing your weight   against a warm floor.
        The loving ground.
            Down down into where all things
                carry you still.

godzilla (2014)

godzilla, o
godzill a o
godz ill a ooo
gods i'll a oooo

he asks
if he can take me out
i say "the new godzilla movie
just came out" he makes a joke
about cum
i laugh, make a
mental note
to add a popcorn combo
to the deal.

in 3D, i slip my hand in the loop
of his waistband,
tease him out: play the game.
he's cum once by the time
the white guy from
malcolm in the middle
dies twenty minutes in.

godzilla, o
godzill a o

god z i'll a oooo
god z i'll aaa o

he cries
when watanabe's
character says
"let them fight"—
not for the same reason as me,
his ex-fiancé stole
his dog & moved
to the philippines.
playing therapist again
godzilla roars in victory
this doesn't get easier,
he's no atomic breath.

godzilla, o
godzill a o

i sneak out the back after
wait thirty minutes
go back in & purchase
another ticket
to watch godzilla

alone,
oh godzilla - ahhh.

r e d

he is inside
he is moving
/fuck yeah/-/fuck yeah/-/fuck yeah/

i am red
he is inside
/does it feel good/

breathe in
/oh babe/
breathe out

his sweat is
pabst blue ribbon
& dispensary dust,
i feel the ridged scar on his right clavicle
trace the tattoo on the lower abdomen of this narrow-hipped boy
this closeness is as near
to being wanted
as i know

/babe does it feel good/
not poised as a question
he strikes deep
finally "stop"
escapes my lips.

he is still inside
red outside
still trying to feel
/oh babe/-/this feels good/-/fuck yeah/

"let's change positions,"
he is quick, hungry
he lets slip the word */mother/*
& i am devoured

he begs for me
to slip a finger inside him
but lacked
the basic decency
to have tidied up inside.
& why let my finger smell
of shit
when he won't listen to
no.

he begs
i apathy
he begs
i become still

he is desperation
& i, necessity.

he begs
whilst inside me
still, i apathy
i am

red:
/fuck yeah/

AKIRA THE HUSTLER

Excerpts from *A Whore Diary*

Sometimes my clients will get really noisy. I'm sure glad that my office door is
properly soundproofed. after all, the police box is right next door!!
A client screamed "Naonosuke!!!!" as he came.
When I asked him about it later,
he said that it was the name of a boy that he had a crush on.

"Sorry for calling out another boy's name when I came...
that was terrible of me," he apologized.
"It certainly was!!" I snapped back.
"I am your love, no, SEX slave!!" a client screamed.
He's right, he is my sex, not love, slave.

A client is standing, or rather leaning.
His enormous frame supported by his hands against the wall.
His body rocks as I spank his ass and fuck him.
He turns his head towards me and screams,

"GOD, I FEEL SO ALIVE"
afterwards, as we were having tea, he was telling me about how completely
exhausted he gets at his desk job.
"When that happens to me I get on my bike and pedal
aimlessly around town. What do you do?" I inquired.

"I come to you," he replied sheepishly, and laughed.

Sometimes I go home after people have said or done
unpleasant things to me. Sometimes I fight with my boyfriend
and my clients help me through it.
Sometimes I learn things about sex at work and
bring them back home. Sometimes I learn about tenderness
at home and develop it into a technique for work.
Sometimes I tire of, or get excited by, the sex at work.
My boyfriend always welcomes me home
and hugs me, with a smile on his face.
My life consists of going, back and forth, between my clients and
my boyfriend. Sometimes it seems like I'm a migrating fish,
swimming down and back a river in flows with money,
camaraderie, love and hate.

A 70-year-old man came to see me. He asked me to lingeringly kiss the nape of his neck. He said that's all he wanted. I asked why. He said that when he was still a teenager, when Japan was still embroiled in the Pacific War, all his friends kept being recruited. He too was up for enlistment. And the one thing that kept him going during the gruelling training that they went through to prepare for battle was the kindness of one of his supervisors, a boy seven years older than he, who had looked after him. Then, one day, this older boy asked him if he could come to his room. When he arrived, the older boy said, "Tomorrow I'm being sent to the front. I may never return. I have one last thing to ask of you." He wanted to spend the night together, he hadn't wanted sex (in a narrow sense) as one might imagine. The boy had simply held him in his arms all night long, caressing his neck with his lips. The older boy never did return. And ever since, this old man had kept the memory of this night, and the warmth and touch of this boy's lips on his neck. Even as he grew older, even through his marriage, he kept coming to boys like me, to relive his memory.

Old man, were my lips warm like his?

The things I've received from my clients:

- A Helmut Lang jean jacket
- an MD player
- fortune cookies from Chinatown
- a Caetano Veloso CD
- a YMCA T-shirt
- love letters
- a down jacket
- a garbage bag full of oranges
- some funky leopard-skin patterned bikini underpants
- a discount ticket for a resort hotel
- a Katharine Hamnett shirt
- an economy pack of lubricant and condoms
- fruitcake
- a yukata dressing gown with yellow sash from Hachijo Island
- rhinestone makeup and organically grown rice condiments
- a well-worn dildo
- a T-shirt from a famous leather bar in New York
- money
- peach flavoured candies
- a sequined Comme des Garçon dress
- a jacket with boa by Helmut Lang
- a Dolce & Gabbana leather jacket
- flyers from gay parties and sex shops in Paris
- tickets to Yumi Matsutoya concert (front row centre!!)
- a CD of Bach hymns
- pants by "Beauty and the Beast"
- a red wig from New York
- an Antônio Carlos Jobim CD
- "Flame" cologne

AMBER DAWN PULLIN

Happy Belated Birthday, whore.

Even my family didn't take the time to tell me that.
It's nice to be remembered. Don't we all want that?

"Saw Your Old Apartment, brought back some good memories for me."

after I moved away,
messages like this
would come in and I'd
masturbate until it hurt.

JUBA KALAMKA

three different streets

I.

You

are a traitor

to your race, gender and culture

(that's what s/h/e typed, verbatim)

among other sundry isms not long before

the camera started rolling

(niggas be *rolling,rolling,rolling* ...)

I received notice   more indictment(s)

that the abstract genitalia diagram of roofing nails on the wall of my loft

would somehow corrupt the mind of my seed

in a manner that the "Street Woman" on our living room wall

(an oil painted in 1968 in a downstate Illinois prison)

managed not to become a Joliet Penitentiary

the 106 miles from Chicago distancing the corruption

Because it's OK and appropriate

for Negro Illustrators to paint

Urban Renewal Murals Encouraging Community Uplift

(Dad's parable: "If you stay in a whorehouse long enough you'll turn a trick, son.")

It's OK as long

As the tricks don't trick us with their trickery

as long as we do not have to imagine

that they might be real people

speak, exposit, cuss

jump out of the varnished mahogany frames

and know where they goin' to
pussypopping at our pre-Kwanzaa dinner party,
causing the Council of Elders
to spill box wine on their leopard print dashikis
mamaspeculation:
["I think he was probably painting a dude."]
as if saying so would make hir less titillating,
make nipples and lines of linae and pubes look less tasty to me
make them somehow less chock full of possibilities
like the way Juneteenth let us know it was gonna happen
(lest we forget)
this be not the Sport and Play of the Asiatic Black Man
the middlesexing that made Elijah Muhammad's dick jump
And got his asthma going
this is our way   *the way*
our ironic and schizoid disgust at our own spectacle[s]
speaking when spoken to
my brain makes scenes that are not heard
but blood taps breakbeats on the rhythmpad inside of my skull.

II.

The party is starting (taps forehead)

up in here   up in here

four 1982 dollars

will buy Italian beef sandwich (bread dipped in au jus)

with a slice of American, ketchup on fries

and a large Suicide with extra ice

and give a bit of time

for the host to stack

penis-shaped soaps and vitamins

while the evening's entertainment

A Reggie Theus lookalike with chest hair like spilled raisins

disrobes in my bedroom

mamasdirective:

("don't come back up the streetlights iz on.")

i hope they tipped well, Reggie

but know they didn't, though they wanted to.

(they could not ... that would be shameless ... and they *are* the shame)

Reg learned me. I want to thank that brotha,

30 years on

for an age-appropriate germ in my twelfth summer

He showed up again later

Courtesy of stepdad's Betamax collection

Sneakpeeks into sex worlds during parent's Saturday overtime

Feature Special Guest Star Mr Johnnie Keyes,

Looking like a Black Nationalist/Pan-Africanist superhero fantasy

Sleeveless White lycra spandex bodysuit

Crotchless with pretty dick swangin' at my face through the screen

Afro flawless, barefoot,

tigertooth necklace nestled on more chestraisins

(I will be his um ... sidekick, yup ... once my balls drop!)

and will fuck alllllll of his run-off pussy
allllllll of dem white girls
just like Jackie Wilson's personal assistant told me he did
back in the day
until that day
I will set the VCR and
will not fast forward through my lessons.

II ½.
I am
somebody
I'm a college graduated bohemian rapnigga
I got a baby mama
but we got in a fight, so now
I got another woman
way over town
with a three chip Sony
oh yeah
and friends doing grainy art school movies with a capital A
on a Fisher-Price PXL 2000
I'm a weekend dad
with lots of free time
and space and time and space
and illmatic head game
(black men don't eat pussy yet, see)
that gets me whines
and crudités
and a spot on an erotica tapeloop, flickering
honey dripping from my nipples
five minutes at a time
in a Barneys New York storefront window display.
No one, (specially baby mama) is the wiser
but i'm learning quickly
if not quite keeping pace with the increasing computational speed
of The School's post production equipment
and the post orgasmic shrinkage
that will eventually
put the power of two in my hand.
It's all fine

fun and games and art and beauty and for The People
until Vaseline lensed scenes with gossamer-draped four-poster bed
Give way to squirting and ass-fisting and Brobdingnagian crotch shots
You and your head is put out and you can't deal with me anymore
And it becomes about "The Children"
As if an eight-year-old boy now two thousand miles away
gives a shit about anything other than
how seldom he sees me
or that his mom needs to give a shit about anything I'm doing
other than whether it's something that will get
the back child support sent to her yesterday through the mail faster.

III.

[*"Is it hot? Check."*]

[*"Do they write hot checks? Naw? Check."*]

then we all good.

and they fitting to posterize this rapfaggot

I'm legendary

I'm nekkid

'cept for my Starbucks apron

piped dress socks, and black Stacy Adams wingtips

they call me El Grande Dark

'cept I like to use my real name

so the kids

so the family

so the chirrens

so them that's in the life

know there's no shame

but that there's a gang of middle class privilege and insulation

That accompanies my altporn collarpopping and academic swag

My lil one [*"papa's going to work tonight."*]

is spit on a skillet.

whip-smart like her mama

[I got another baby mama]

Who be a fried squirrel 'n' beans eatin' Missouri trash girl

With a raft of hiding from DCFS trepidation cum terror

Inherited from her own mama.

Unlike my talented tenthian protonegro self

me and my 1964-bits of civil right

Mixblood dyke trashgirl attorneys know

That the law is what is *done*

So she tell me to bring home stories

Teach them chirren well

Swang that dick
Wire that grocery and rent money
watch your black ass, baby
'cause we love your black ass
Be careful in tour with that gang of hoes
Especially when riding through Scottsboro
And hug them
because I love them hoes, too
and love comes quick.
coins come in a hurry.
we git it done
no waiting on student union admin to cut us loot
my boy is now old enough to guess what his dad's steez is
but we still have the formal conversation
as I'm hyper conscious of leaving things unsaid
["*yeah, dad, I kinda guessed from the spines of the dvds on the shelf.*"]
I'm getting to that age now
summer short suits, piped dress socks
mints and toothpicks in shirt pocket
unlit Kool Menthol rapidly bobbing on the bottom lip
'cause I'm too busy shit-talking to light it
Driving it home
leaning back
burgundy sedan be immaculate
Egyptian Musk freshener from the record store
hanging from the rearview
leather seats polished and
Important Papers tucked in the passenger side sun visor
["you know what this is, boy?"]
["*yeah, dad ... issa check.*"]
["it ain't jussa check, boy."]

Teenage eyes roll like Vegas slots.
["*what is it, then?*"]
["it's a car note."] ["it's from a *job.*"] ["it's work."]
["it's *always* work."] ["it's good."] ["it's real ..."]
["and *fuck anybody* that *ever* tries to tell you different."]

Ode to a hooker, without the usual vocabulary

Long before women were monsters she swam
in the blood like a fish, long-toothed and strange,
something out of mud, indigo-eyed,
stirring on ocean floor dappled sun
on her murmur skin and somersault body.

some unrefined substance
made subtle by more turns of the wheel. She grew tired
of waiting. She's the sickle-edged moon,
mean-mouthed, no easy lay. Her whole life a barfight,
her frogsong voice forgetting nothing.

When she went on two feet she was the owl
on four, a mama wolf. Now having transcended toes
altogether she dabbles in root & stem
& leaf, snaggletoothed as time,

wearing the night only.

Meat

Someday i will write a sex work memoir,
and title it *Meat* at first glance it will
appear to be about the commodification
of the sacred female form (or,
like, dicks) but really it will be
about how well i have eaten
since i started whoring: great
ribbons of sausage links, tides
of bone broth. Meat: how my
cells murmur in anticipation of
the butcher's pink paper wrappers,
a red name that shivers on my tongue
& quickens to the marrow with
pleasure at every bite.

fifth floor walk-up.

There is a seizure of you
　　　　/ inside me / / /
mouth charcoal
gargling gag gag　gag gag gaggaggaggaggaggaggaggaggaggaggag
but you have paid me by the hour
and we have twenty minutes
more.

Here, humans have spandex skin
local businesses branding backs.

Here, sky sutures mountains between clouds
and there are thirteen shades of
tree and soil.

While five floors up
in parking garage in suburban vehicle,
my knees bruise against upholstered floor.

After, you put mint in your mouth as though
my sucking your dick changed your breath
somehow.

With you, there are no words beyond
what you order, which is the same each time.

I am fast-food menu minus discounts and
dipping sauces

I am still pulling out carpet threads
from parts of my skin
I have given away.

Later, thunder & homework
& formulating words with an aftertaste
of the cash register between your legs.

kind of like citrus

1.
I didn't understand why you needed to pay me.
You had jesus christ abdominal muscles and all your hair.

You were young enough to remind me that you hadn't married yet
but considered proposing to your girlfriend who lives long distance.

You told me my hair was pretty and *I* was pretty but not like
your girlfriend is pretty;
she is beautiful, you said.

All of your furniture matched and you had fancy pillows on your bed
and I wondered how long-distance this girlfriend really was.

I only saw you that one time and I can still remember
that your semen tasted expensive.

Like your tan.
Like citrus.

2.

You purchased your cigarettes off the internet.

Each time you tried to slide your spit into my mouth, I turned my head.
Your tongue, like cured salami. Like nicotine-drenched faucet.

You had the smallest cock of any man I had ever seen and I was grateful for this.
I closed my eyes and imagined it as a clit as a poem as a Lou Reed song as a mountain.

With your dick inside me, I read every book by Kathy Acker, meditated to Philip
Glass, alphabetized my grocery list and record collection.

I cut myself in half, zigzagged and charred flesh while you
pumppumppumped
and I pretended to notice.

3.

You were the last one.

The ink on my wrist told you I was a poet, so you asked me to read you
    something.
I chose the queerest piece I had because I wanted you to feel left out.

When you asked if I was gay, I segued into menu option number four.

Outside, the storm covered everything in snow
Inside, I was ice ~~melting~~ disappearing from the weight of you.

You kept calling me your girlfriend
even after you walked me three blocks to an ATM to extract cash.

Called me girlfriend as you linked your nude, callused fingers
against my gloved ones.

Called me girlfriend as I watched you count all those twenties
before folding them up and hiding them in my ripped jacket pocket.

In a thing in a place where some stuff happened

Everyone says it smells like ketchup
They say just close your eyes and when he spreads you open,
you are in Piha with black sand and volcanic ghost beneath you
—just let him in it's easier this way—

Have you ever worn your bones inside out,
dipped tongues over lungs to taste the weight of your breaths,
you can feel this, just close, just close your eyes
it will be over it will be over it will be over.

You first learned how with that boy in his bedroom and that movie
starring Reese Witherspoon in the background,
while somewhere in another room,
his mother whistled something ironic.

Years later, you can still taste that boy's dirt
that boy's sperm
that boy's fingernails digging into your scalp
pushing you onto onto onto him.

You still don't know where to put your allergies when strangers
sit their itches between your knees; no one needs to know about
that time you sewed a Santoku knife behind your teeth and
just bit. Down.

Everyone says it will go away,
~~it it it it it it it it it it it it it it it~~
you will turn invisible,

your skin will be too loose to hold onto,
no one will try again.

But you say there is no such thing or place
where this stuff
suddenly stops
and you are no longer evidence to break into.

STRAWBERRY

3 strong pairs of hands

My friends literally perform alchemy
Take the agony turn it to ferocious manic joy
Take the numbness turn it to healing tears
and buoyant laughter

We prowl the night, pissing in bushes shouting lyrics
Dancing wildly as gulls and heron fly overhead
There is an emptiness that can only be filled by this for now
By shows and long afternoons in the garden, late
nights and early mornings

They turned a bruise into a blue rose
turned my hunger into immortality
Took my fear and spun it into red wool
that trails behind me so I can find my way back
When i am *oh so fucking* afraid that my feet will take
me to the atm, to rock bay then to the nearest bathroom
I call
I run
I am saved, hallelujah hail mary

My friends literally perform alchemy
with a smoke dangling from their lips, sweat drying on their skin
We thrash, lose time, explode with unbelievable pressure,
tension turning repression into violence, that violence so loving

that an elbow to the jaw feels like a kiss on the forehead
When I fall, three strong pairs of hands heave me up
If you fall, *we will catch you*

I wish I wrote more, wish I used a condom
I wish nights like that could stay suspended in time forever
Pressed up against the ceiling of a morning so determined to come
I follow tangled red wool back to my bed, lay warm
safe
bruised
and sore
grateful i didn't die at fifteen

A John's Funeral

Friend and I were catching up on what life has become for us without sex work
We laugh at the similarities of not dating or getting into a relationship
"forever alone" we joke
We talk about how neither of us has had sex since we exited
4–5 years for me 3–4 years for her
Sex for us both has always been a transaction of some sort
She then asks *"Did you get the message about* ██████ *passing?"*
I nod and laugh thinking about this John
We talk about how he was a decent trick who we both saw
twice a week, we laugh about how strict he was
on about which days of the week he'd meet us
Monday mornings and Thursday afternoons for her
Friday early evenings and Sunday afternoons for me
She asks if we should attend the funeral with a giggle
I think to myself   *"Is there etiquette to attend a Trick's funeral?"*
just cause he was a good fuck, paid well and great cock for an older man
I get lost in this thought, my friend shakes me out the rabbit hole
"Wanna go?"   I laugh, they start sharing memories
We will go up, *"Here we are to pay our respects to this man, he paid fucking well*
and tipped too. also a great fuck" my friend adds   *"Great cock too"*
In a fit of laughter, we fall into one another

RAVEN SLANDER

West End Sex Workers Memorial

In the back lane
off Davie Street
I light a cigarette
No smoking
  indoors anymore
Fishnets & tall boots
I like what I think
they're thinking
  the passers-by
Inhaling flashes
of cities & of nights
street corners & strolls
of excitement & anticipation
of men in cars
of money coming money going
of waiting around & smoking

Truly I don't know what
they're thinking
Times have changed
I'm older now
  Not as skinny
  dope skinny, it's true

Then, I wore crop tops & tight tights
so they could see what I had
cuz I knew what they wanted
   the chasers, the johns
Taunts
being spat at
bad dates
getting ripped off
roughed up & beaten up
   I remember too
But we rode the night
trannys on the tranny stroll
shit talkers & straight shooters
rivals & thieves
spotters & seraphims
companions & lovers
cocaine & courage
heroin & bareback

We rode the night until
the genocide of indifference
& conniving knives of hatred
   disappeared us all
Here in the back lane
just a block from the newly erected
West End Sex Workers Memorial
a tall pillar
a lighted crimson beacon
a bronze plaque
Finally this for us

In the end
a *red-light* tomb

A car slows
my breath sharpens
I wonder
& light another cigarette

We are the girls who die unnoticed

I was once in a newspaper
with a long Roberto Cavalli dress and lollipops
on the bed of the man who would rape me
when I told him *I do not love you anymore.*
I had fake hair and a dress I would only wear
to show my back and ass and tears.
In the newspaper I am quoted saying *being a whore
is less harsh on my feet than being a waitress.*
I keep my high heels on when the men knock at the door
kiss them on their mouth or cheek
wait for bills
and then take them off
so they are always shiny and new.
And it is true
being a whore is less harsh for me
than picking strawberries in a field
I made 20 dollars a day picking strawberries
then came home covered in dirt
smelling sweat and sweet.
Being a whore is less harsh for me than waking up at 4
to write in big bold letters *bacon*
The cook made bacon and scrambled eggs and peanut butter toast
for men coming in Les Princesses d'Hochelaga
to watch sports and porn and drink coffee.
They'd ask for bacon and a picture of my tits

before they struggled to build castles and skyscrapers.
I was once in a newspaper.
I wore mermaid eyeshadow.
I'm not dead yet.
I do Lego with my kids and cry and say sorry
too many times or not.
I'm not dead yet.
A man raped me because I was not his doll.
He had scars over his arms and he used to tell me it hurt
when we were watching documentaries or war movies.
I don't remember if I was hurt when he shoved his cock in my ass.
When I was picking strawberries I was scared of spiders.
I'm not scared of a lot of things.
Firemen are called when I make cookies and it's fine.
I don't do cookies anymore.
I don't cherish his scars and his wine.
I'm scared to die unnoticed.
Like any girl who is healing.

A letter to my body

I left for so long
I got confused
I thought someone else lived here.
No. Not someone.
Anyone.
Anyone who laid claim.
Planted a flag.
Put down roots.
I didn't know I was an option.

And then I did.
It was beautiful.
I organized timeshares!
I can be here!
You can be here!
He can be here!
She can be here!
They can be here!
THEY can be here!

Just let me know.
There. Is. Plenty. Of. Wiggle. Room.
And I'm very accommodating.
But I'm shy.
I'm going to go.

Tell me when you're done.

I'll sweep and mop.

Patch holes and cracks.

GET THIS GIRL READY FOR MARKET

I was gone for so long.

I got confused.

I thought other people should be allowed to stay here.

I thought this was a vacation rental.

I didn't realize this was a home.

This no hostel.

There is no vacancy.

Only one occupant.

All year round.

No sublease.

Hello, I'm sorry,

I'm home.

SACRED COLLECTIVE

Collaboratively Voiced by Sacred

We are a proud people. Sex work does not make us weak.
Living a life of fear and degradation, unknown
The Indigenous woman sex worker is the lowest
of the low on the totem pole.
Invisible,
divisible,
disposable,
disposable,
disposable,
Remains found on pig farmer's land.
Disappeared from the highway of tears.
We are women and have feelings too.
The lives of Indigenous sex workers
are very challenging,
dangerous,
unyielding.
We work our way through.
We are survivors.

Dear Trauma

I used to think of you
                    as a burden
a heavy thing that I had to lug around
a thing I had to explain to people
                    I got intimate with.
You weren't an excuse but
        you were a barrier.

I thought I'd be different
somehow better off
                    without you.
I thought if I could learn to shake you off
                    or isolate you somehow
                    I would be a more whole person.

If I could get over you I could move on.

But I've realized I'm grateful to you.
You are a gift I didn't want.
You have informed so many of my decisions.
You kept me safe and maybe kept me alive.
You are my secret weapon, and your sibling
        dissociation
                    is my super power.
You've taught me to act sooner

and more decisively. You've shortened
the length of time it takes for me to know
when shit is bad and needs to change.

I didn't always trust you but it doesn't matter
because you were always there
doing your thing
getting me out and through.
I cannot shake you, and that has to be okay.
You have helped me survive
the worst and hardest moments of my life.

Beloved Boy

His was a soft-spoken voice.
I rarely took him seriously when he would say, "I'm a man
trapped in a beautiful woman's body," I thought he was only
being clever. But the more I tried
to be a perfect whore, the greater I saw him
as I stared at my reflection in the all of the mirrors
in all the green rooms of pornography
sets I've ever fucked in. My tits

compressed into latex dresses and lingerie
always a size too small to accentuate my ass and B-cup chest.
I looked beautiful, like a woman I would want to befriend.
As much as I wanted to be
that person, I couldn't drown out
the tiny voice in my head. For a few hours, for my directors
and co-performers, I could pretend. It was easy when they were
queer women. The blank stares
wouldn't wash over their faces
when I told them my pronoun is he/his and they/them.
When I was performing with men, I wouldn't bother
revealing who I am. I would swallow

their misogynistic
and racist microaggressions and feign a poor excuse for a Japanese accent
as I was instructed so I could stack bread. "Just make enough money

as a woman until you can finally be a man," my intuition
encouraged. For some sex workers, hustling
is their daily sustenance until the day they peacefully rest. For me, at least
back then, it was a means to an end. I couldn't believe that I could gain
any semblance of success as a baby boy
too broke to transition. This is what a boy
becoming a man looks like. When they open their legs
for their femme sex worker friends. This is a man whose gender
is never threatened by wearing iridescent nail polish

and, on occasion, his wife's leggings
and undergarments. A couple of years ago, I didn't understand
that I don't need to defend who I am. I did not yet know that love
is a strange grace. Love is an angel
who visits the evening
you choose to sell your spirit. This strange grace comes to you
in dreams of your ancestors, the eskrimadoras, beheading the colonizers
who stole your land and the name of your elders.
It's a strange love that comes to you
when you are ready to live the rest of your life being someone else,
someone who you are not, someone who will kill you and those who came
before you if you chose to be like them. It kisses
your third eye, caresses your crown, and tells you that
who you are is more than okay.
You are queen beloved. When this angel visits, she will look like
every hustler you've ever adored. My angel,
she is my community, and she is my wife.
When my hair starts to grow in unfamiliar places and my skin gets tougher
from testosterone, I will not forget the lessons I learned from my ho family.

When I'm a seahorse daddy
and my wife's baby is inside me,
I will remember how whores don't let public mockery stop their glow. Hustlers
with pride keep hustling. *Ang anak ko*, I'll tell my child, *you come from generations
of hustlers who hustled so that you could be here today.*
Be proud, I'll whisper to my belly.
You are my whole world, mi amor.
You are beloved.

ANNOYING HH

productive
        discomfort
is knowing
your work

        will be
constructed as

marked
        as dirty.
adam wants
to make
a sexy
movie

to visibilize
our personal
history,

never forget
how time
passes

in the annoying
half-hour

do whatever
for a dollar

150?
head so
good

he says
i give
him life,
hunty

but
i get paper
and a sticky
tissue—

milky
moksha

my labour
of transition

stuck in
a cycle.

i'm doing
what it takes

to get out,
i give out
my gentle
parts—

scatter
everywhere.

is it choice
or survival?

      an act.
can we
watch it
together?

can we
even begin
to describe
what a soul is?

Playing

i.
my arm flailed on your
mother-in-law's hospital bed   knocked the whiskey
glasses off bedside table, then the glass
table top as you
relaxed yourself into me
"i'm just playing"   i won't wake deeper
i party and play with a former escort manager
who is playing my party his way into my
substance

pause before cellphone
then wash my options into purgatory
till there is nothing to decide

ii.

i'm just playing your defeated cum onto my lips
you'll never enjoy a blow job the same
you won't let out a sincere moan of pleasure or release
your sex is a tool
a collar you broke yourself into   i hold the leash
but i'm just playing

i'm in love with a hooker
She is my girl
after pinning her tense throat   fucking her dry ass
i ask her if she has been hurt
She says yes of course   shrugs as she sinks away
further into the glossy mattress beneath me

i'm just playing an eight-year marriage
the kids asleep on their beds in the windows
on the other side of the penthouse

As to divide our speech exists

i.

as to divide   our speech exists
we hear out
the harsh passings of the wet street
we touched our questions into each other
my tender thumb and lips expound
uncertain urges to your deltoid
explicate my headtilt   her shyness her locked

crouch our shaggy heads over the table
draw with a pen on the seams of button-up shirt
hold my hand as we clench our jaws

patience is a comedown
the burn in your back from a rest
left unattended

ii.

as to divide   our speech exists
we're touching our questions into each other
my lips and tender thumb shyly whisper
uncertain urges to your deltoid
explicate my headtilt   her bashful her locked jaw

mount me on the awkward couch breaks down
dog scratched leather outside her bedroom
carelessly big a room spreads apart sections

i'm gonna cry about this when it's raining
i'm holding your fists in my sweaty palms
a silver lining in my jacket
flakes onto my T-shirt when it's hot

Revival at the Pillow Talk Lounge

She brings the thrum of bees with her, ·
      dances beneath cherry lights & the speaker's
thump-pulse groove. She sings her
      bruises to the beer-soaked walls, honey-alto
rattling: *Won't you take me*
      to Funky Town / won't you take me ...
She drops low—
whispers sugar in my ear,
      my folded bills sweat
between her breasts,
      dozens of men pound the stage,
I am damp in my dress, swollen,
twitching in my seat.
            She just shimmies, shimmers
snaps her fingers—purple talons and that
tone—head thrown back, curses loosed,
seven-league heart unlaced,
      frenzy in her hips,
this rapture is for God
not some recycled room in a strip club,
      not this bend of the Chattahoochee—
waters writhing through red clay and dreck,
      licking the club's back door, hoarding
skeletons in cement shoes,
      blue girls with their pimp's names

tattooed inside their lips,
> dope fiends and snitches,
failed hit men and the damned—
>> this is not the house of God
yet there she is.
> Whipping around the pole,
back arched, heart bare—She is
the second coming,
> and dear God
I believe.

muchfuckdyke (Horticulture)

Daisy dukes   through
town after soaking her skirt on a dare.
she's   off, but often offering: doesn't scare
me. friendly enough and grew
bankable breasts; let me cop my first feel. promised head.
Amber only bumps for bread.

lackadaisical me; i dream daisies.
i sold my whole heart to every
flower she ever had the pleasure to pluck.
"i love you too," she bloomed, "but i'll never have quite as   much
to sell." darling, you're already more than enough.
us'll survive each scurrying scurrilous faggot-fucking   fuck.

our discourse parodies prophecy:
"fuck the police." "i *do*. i'm banking on it." but Chicago
cops lock up more gay whores than rapists.   So.
if we piss you off, you can piss on me—
that is if pissing gets you off. tell me what you like:
fifty extra or a glock. show
me your carnage incarnate. Amber's bi. Daisy's just a   dyke.
who will ever really know.

(Perfect flowers have both stamens and pistils.)

Countess
(hospital ward)

Daisy's daffy: girl has all the time in the world
and spent near none on a sulk.
    [like lilacs or lilies she used to lilt. then Everymister bloom
    his bloody balloon.
    crept cross her canals. pried and pinned and pumped and forced with fists
    her fluttering points
    until barely could either breathe and up she blew. hurled.]
come evening, Amber's out and so jejune
                   do talk
                      the two:

"Yes, i will die dim, insides fallow fields full and empty
of Everyman—without return from Sir's insurmountable mount."
"for the best, i guess: returns a little death; not only   death
is death is bigger than big." "I jests at that (what pests me):
i wake each day aquake in mourning dew; always of sorrows
do i lose my count.
and yet: today awake am i." "tomorrow?"
                    "we can bet again on breath."

i need know one brute truth, oh ambling Ambers all:
are you ashes? or in scarlet swatch plumes
will plummet upwards you upon your words?
(says Everyman:) "come now—upwards." "through such thick brume?"
    now PEP's in your step. you'll not be sick more; ought it may teach
you how to grieve each
hospital, however indomitably inhospitable to whores.

and i'm here;
i'm here.
though for all you've fallen floral, come here, Daisy dear: i'll be your ward.

Fantasy Breakers

An author who writes about her intoxicating yet toxic
dalliance with the work is applauded for her literary courage.

She shines in pages where I do not find my reflection.
Her racy scenarios keep heartbeats fast and curious
for those who see us as a consumable edge. No other industry
is written about with such possessed intrigue.

I throw the book. Light the candles. Check my makeup. Return to work.
When I am not his escape, I still don't feel safe from the law.

I'm swamped with acting gigs and the backend of business
is an ever-evolving door of flash assessment while I perfect the craft
of edging but I'm sure as hell bored of caring for men. If there was
a honeymoon period, I batted my lashes for the cash and the color amber
quickly turned green. The most titillating part is when I lay
on the massage table or couch or bed after he leaves, relaxed and paid
although a little bit greasy as I wait for the sensations of men's desire
to wear off my lithe body and I call my best friend to humorously vent.

you know that day when every client is named steve?
you know that day when every client is named steve
and wants the same service?

you know when you wish you could speak about your job

in a normal setting with normal working people, a bank teller, or a cashier
and not have to preemptively consider their possible invasive inquiries
or perhaps even worse their silence
a micro to the macro silence

a sex worker all at once invisible and iconic
liberator and gold digging demon.

you know when you just don't feel like lying?
you know when sex workers feel like everything to you?
you know when you can't get the cologne off your hair?

Boat Show

on our backs we build campfires, wreck trains, track ourselves

(semblance of bedroom)

on our backs, an American heredity of forage and predatorial scout

skin plowed to plant a piece of hair, a plunged handle,
something plastic catches the light)

the scaffold creates a laboratory of balanced sound

do you think you'll be more beautiful once you start screaming?

it's only the bones of it
it's only things we're doing

by June, the mapping of our bodies rubs like boat hulls.

the same body pixilated and splayed
sits across from a book on 18th
just up from the park
all openings visible

in the woman, the corpus callosum is thick as a tunnel

pretense of sensitivity as female
another orchid comparison
splayed labia pinned like a beetle

another square of muscle becomes immune
when I begin screaming, I am more beautiful.

Study

We keep naming ourselves. We keep time,

we keep track

we keep
we keep
we count

the tiles in the lobby bathroom at the Mark Hopkins Hotel are
black and white ceramic, are 5 by 5 inches. grabbed jackets and
stacks we flatten ones and fives against the lip of the sink

graze the petals of display bouquets, step out into the night,
know our purchasing power.

On another day,

I'd make it more sad. Believing in grammar, I'd make it sadder.

Give Alice a necklace and make her touch it,
make her move the pendant up
and down on the chain, absentmindedly, looking
out a plate glass window

Behind her I'd put a bachelor party and say it's her birthday.

Say she's turning twenty-nine and has to quit
soon. Say she's nineteen and faking it, say she's thirty-two

and won't quit. Say money sticks to her skin. Say it's 2:30 a.m. and she wants
to go home and eat potato chips

Say money sticks to her skin

What Alice knows: object equals construct leads to
ownership

Her hands sweat.   My hands sweat.   We hold on.   Say *I*. Say *I
am*.
Stiletto, shoe or knife?

In the suite on the 37th floor there is a floral print couch, floor to ceiling window,
white carpet scattered with cups and money, two men sit on the edge of the bed
debating what they'll pay for.

One of them says to me, my breasts in his face *where do you go to college*

He doesn't wait for an answer, turns to his friend and says:
all strippers go to college

If you open your wallet, I'll let you believe it.

We say *art.*
We say *dance.*
We say pay me.

costume as in play, club as in
belong. There is no alone.
Purchase as in: a place to stand.

Here:

The work made us, but first—

are you listening—

We made the work.

At the bachelor party, the men avoid touching each other.

They want to.
They want to,
they want

They lean on the balcony rail with blue cups of whiskey
and soda and look
out at the city and pretend
to see only the girl and pretend
not to see anything.

Their skins are sticky with hope,
with lotion that smells of oranges.

They've taken their shirts off to lie
on the floor with money
over their mouths.

Outside the floor-to-ceiling window, the city is so new,
                                        it must be America.

Talking Sexy

he framed it up for me
explaining what I would do
what he would do
who we were doing it to
how hot it was going to be
how perfect it was.

In the fantasy
we were
boyfriend
girlfriend
and we had a little girl.

"Don't worry.
I would never ever actually do this
in real life,
I don't have any kids
I promise
I don't have kids."

I blanked
chain smoked
did my job.

I could recognize his voice
like a grandparent
not speaking for years

he described everything
what he was doing to her
how far he could get inside of her
how small she was

then he wanted to switch
begged me to take over

If anyone heard the things I said
I don't think I could look them in the eye anymore.

When he finished
he kept saying,
"I love you
I love you
I love you
I wish I had a girlfriend like you
I can't wait to call you again
I love you
I love you."

I know
he had an amazing time
I know
I did a really good job

I did a good job. I'm good at it.

my life in public service

in 1992: $6/hour minimum wage, rent for a one-bedroom apartment in East Vancouver cost $500/month, full-time studies at community college cost $500/semester

$40/blow job, $60/lay, $80/half and half

in 2008: $8/minimum wage, rent for a one-bedroom apartment in East Vancouver cost $900/month, full-time studies at community college cost $1000/semester

KAY KASSIRER

Sex Work Client

sex work client does not understand
exactly how sex work
works

his sugar baby website profile says "no escorts"
I message him anyways

after all this job is more acting than sex
more affirmations than orgasms

sex work client does not know he is a client
prefers to think himself boss
prefers to think himself in charge

as if I did not decide how much money I will be paid for my labour here tonight
as if he did not just buy me steak dinner, roasted yukon potatoes, and three
    glasses
of 1995 vieux châteaux rouge
as if he did not just bring me a brand-new dress
and a pair of knock off jimmy choos

sex work client isn't afraid
to tell me what it means
to be a woman
says he relates

to the feminine struggle
he says I should wear skirts
and stilettos more often

sex work client pays for sex
because spending money is easier
than adding up everything
his toxic masculinity
has cost him

call back

I navigate you with three texts, wait 15 minutes on the porch
to quick freeze the fear of you: wpgfitguy44.

My nerves dull when you tell me I'm *pretty*.
I pretend this is something I haven't
already figured out. Stairs crack loudly beneath
me as your peachy hand leads me to a mattress.
Piss yellow. Oddly fitting.

The texture of your mouth wraps me in cigarettes, booze and sugary sweets.
My tongue works quickly.

Your hand on lips, nails press, eyes truly busy with my fat chest.
The weight of hips push you deep through the floor boards. Fuck you.

I disturb your flickering eyes. This cums with a loss
of admiration, infatuation, longing, fleeting dusk.

I roll my doughy body from your beaten pan.
Sticky, fucked, glistening, bake me at 300.

Fingering what you've left for me?
Awe, you should've.

SASCHA

aspartame baby

You could say I had everything I needed
but nothing I wanted. Like the velvet pleated
A-line skirts, swingy, heavy, and navy blue,
in the shop windows on Beacon Hill. Like the gloves
made of burgundy leather that melts like butter
under your fingertips when you slide them on, lined with fur.
I'd become the person who could acquire
one finery after another
Barring that, I'd impersonate her.

I come from a line of Jewish Madams,
bootleggers, boxers, and gamblers. Everything is up for grabs
in America. I'd be like Marilyn Monroe, cooing and wiggling for riches,
like the busty, puffy-lipped cartoon gold diggers in *Playboy* magazine,
with their minks and martinis and heels. My gender is diamonds.
My gender is pearls.
I was young and rosy-cheeked, but wily with a WiFi connection,
clicking for surrogate grandpas to SPOIL ME, SPOIL ME, SPOIL ME.

It was the long con,
and my first disguise was a dopey co-ed
with a goyed-up name, who just wanted to try East Coast oysters
on the rooftop of the Prudential, for the very first time.
I walked out with four bills and not even the breath
of a man on my skin. So I did it again. I spent

each weekend with Jeffs, Phils, and Garys, innumerable Daves,
keeping my cards close to the chest. I spent
their dirty cash on the softest suede
boots, on the kind of perfumes
that *take you on a journey*, that really

Tell a story. Mine was about a girl who refused
her station in life, who was spitting mad and covetous,
enough to fool every sad bastard in town
with the promise of flesh.
One widower looked just like Shrek. A real toad,
his face slick with longing, I slipped off
my shoulder strap and made sure he could smell my skin.
Then got an "emergency" text from a friend. In the end,

I redistributed their filthy lucre like a girl Robin Hood,
swapping my frayed tights for Wolfords whenever I could,
pushing scallops into my big mouth like Ursula,
all schemes and appetite
listening to their same boring fishing stories
with money, money on my mind.

Before he died, my real grandfather
gave me this safety tip: Always look for the nearest exit.
I found it in the thick white envelopes slid discreetly across the tables
of hotel cocktail lounges, I found it in the hopeful and lonely eyes
of my marks. I always got away.

I will exit the debt and scarcity my generation inherited,
I will demand lily bouquets, red brocade dresses, gold truffles,
if it means that I'm a rapacious and cunning little tease.

After all, I was given several years
of public school acting lessons.
After all, I was given so many desires for so many things
just out of my reach

like downtown at Christmastime, windows alight and shimmering,
with always the possibility, but never the prize,
tinsel glinting on concrete, strewn from an empty box.
And me—pink neon lights flashing in the shape of a woman.

Industry

Want really classy slim young
white girl want natural natural
natural enhanced. Natural enhanced.
32D 34C. Natural D. Natural D cup!
Slim young brunette with a natural D cup!
5'6" 110 5'6" 120 5'11" 130 5foot95
Tiny. Tiny. Tiny natural body. Tiny natural body
Super slim cheerleader body, got that nice
Perky enhanced D cup. B cup. 32B 36D
Slim cute blonde all natural C. Smart
And classy, pretty and witty top-notch service,
great GFE! 5:30 Destiny 6 o'clock Bliss
25–36, 5'6" 140, *super* curvy body!
Slender body pretty face! 5'11" tight
And toned tight tight tight tight tight tight toned
Not natural Ds, enhanced please. Not 125
want tiny please. Not 27, new young please.
Want great service want GFE. Enhanced and perky,
Open minded and friendly, bubbly and sweet!
New to the business, busty and sweet!
5'6" 120, fun college girl brunette Japanese
young cute natural natural enhanced. Natural
enhanced. Service with a smile and perfect reviews
I want really classy. Young. Fresh. New.

KEVA LEE

Triple F Threat

I am Mistress Keva.
I am a professional dominatrix
an Asian woman
an Asian dominatrix. I am an Asian sex worker
which invariably makes me the object of the Asian fetish.

Kink and race are so intertwined I would not know how
                                        to separate the two.
I have played
the Japanese schoolgirl poking fun of her nerdy White teacher
the Dragonlady from *Terry and the Pirates*
while sticking needles in my captor's balls
and the trafficked sex worker seeking revenge on her pimp

I like to think that over time, I have learned to exploit
the stereotypes
now able to navigate through them with a bit of humor

        Here begins my story of the three Fs of my domme world.

i. Food

My first kinky food experience started Valentine's Day
I wanted the night to be romantic. Tea lights
were lit down the hallway leading to a bed
strewn with flower petals.

Completely naked except for a whip cream bikini.
It was all very *Varsity Blues* circa 1999.

Reality was not as sexy and fantasy-like as I thought it would be.
My ex-girlfriend took one lick of my boob and all I could smell
was the dairy on her breath for the rest of the night. I asked her
to brush her teeth but she said she was "too lazy." I held
my breath the whole night trying not to smell
the sweet sourness of whip cream.

Years later I was in a tiny bathroom willed with the same sticky
sweet smell of dairy filling the air
My first food sploshing session

     I was wearing a marching band uniform.
     My client lay in the tub, also in his marching band uniform.
The role-play and session first started in another dungeon room.
I was in the cool marching band and part of the cool drum line.
He was a nerdy band geek from an opposing school and played the clarinet
or bassoon or perhaps some other woodwind instrument.
We were in some sort of game show competition and I kept winning.
(I actually pretended to play the game show host as well.)

     "And the winner is ... Keva I Lee!" I announced.
     "And the winner is ... Keva I Lee. And now I'm going to spit on you!"
     "And the winner is ... Keva I Lee! And now I'm going to faux fuck you
          in the ass
     with this large buttplug over your marching band uniform."

This went on for quite some time until
the last and final round. He lost again
ended up in the bathtub still wearing his marching band uniform.
There I cracked raw eggs on his head, I dumped cups of Jell-O
pudding on him. I sprayed whip cream. The food was
the humiliation
complete with me peeing
on him for the finale.
I started to learn more about kink
and food. Humiliation and food.
Food and fetish.

ii. Fetish

This role-play started with my client playing the grocery delivery boy. We had corresponded
via email beforehand and I told him to bring bread, grapes, bananas and cookies.
He was adamant about bringing chow mein. I kept saying I did not want chow
mein until I realized, *Oh ... he wants a Chinese girl eating Chinese noodles and spitting them
into his mouth.* I call this the baby bird fetish. Basically to chew something up and
then spit it into the submissive's mouth. He wanted the baby bird food as well as
any of my fluids—snot, spit, mucus, pee—whatever I could or would drop into
his mouth.

During the session,
I spat the noodles into his mouth.
I even decided to up the Chinese ante
and made dim sum with my snot.
I blew my nose into the bread
and told him it was dim sum.

"Here's *ha gow*" (shrimp dumpling)

"Here's a *cha siu bao*" (barbecue pork bun)

I even stuffed grapes in my nose and blew them out like snot rockets (there is no Cantonese word for this). He loved all of it. He was shaking his leg like a dog. He enjoyed the session so much he decided to come back next month for a follow-up session, but this time he wanted me to spit food in his mouth and fart in his mouth. I took this on as a challenge and accepted. I brought along my best friend.

We prepared all day for the session.

We told him to come at the very end

of the day when we would likely be

our gassiest from eating cheese all day.

He was to bring more cheese, along with coffee, the usual grapes, bread and bananas. We did the baby bird feeding, but when it was time to fart we could not muster one out. And we tried. We seriously tried. We were doing yoga moves, the downward dog, the plough, the cat and cow. Now imagine two Asian girls dressed in black lingerie doing yoga moves in the middle of a dimly lit dungeon floor while an old White guy on his hands and knees wags his leg like a tail waiting to suck out their farts. That was us. But we just could not do it. We could not fart. When he left I realized it was performance anxiety.

A whole day of cheese with no results.

And just as my session ended with farts

this story also ends with farts.

iii. Farts

(Even though I have written about farts) Fart requests
are not a usual everyday occurrence. As I said before, I take it
as a challenge. Sometimes I just pretend that I am about to fart

or threaten to fart.

He was a professional singer, both in real life and in the role-play scenario.
He had an arrogance about him that was quiet and annoying. To him, all Asian
Mistresses in the scene were my friends and we were all interchangeable.

His email complimented me on my grace
and poise, but not without stating that he should know
because of his past dating adventures with Asian pageant queens.
He was tall, lanky and White. He was completely nondescript
aside from his specific role-play scenario. I was to play his wife.
The night before we were supposed to be at a cocktail party.
I caught him singing to another woman. In a fit of jealousy
I confront him about his indiscretions. I become so angry
that I make him sing for me. And he actually sang for me. We were
sitting on the bed in the boudoir setting of the dungeon and he sang
for me. Still wearing his suit and tie, his voice was soothing
in a piano lounge sort of way. It was like Barry Manilow
and Nat King Cole. As he sang for me, I pretended to become
even more enraged and jealous. I could not believe
he used his beautiful voice to sing to another woman.
I loved his voice so much
I only wanted it for myself.

> "How could you sing to another woman? You should only be singing to
> me!"
> He apologized but that only made me angrier until
> I threatened to piss and fart in his mouth.
> "Look at you with your mouth wide open. Hold that vowel longer.
> What if I just piss right in your mouth right now?"

As I taunted him I told him to sing louder, to hold his notes longer, to sing into
my ass. Just as I bend over to tell him to sing again, I feel him nuzzle his nose

between my ass cheeks and out from between my ass I hear him sing. "Unforgettaaabbllle ... That's what you are ..."

On & Off the Job

In halcyon days

your thumb
pressing against
my spine

I had

this tendency
to reserve
my pleasure

    On the job

    If
    my body
    had
    a
    Nixonian
    plan
    I threw in
    a Mona Lisa
    smile

What's with
these activists
telling me?

    "No children
    at this table"

    I
    was
    there.

Three years later

    Deprived
    of something
    I hadn't
    always
    wanted

    When you held
    my hand
    without
    touching

I discovered
that
needing it
is better
than anything

It wasn't
because
I was ready
to start
working
again.

The grandiose
buried in
my soul
playing
no role
in this

My body
was ready
for us—

My theory.

But you
protected
my heart

and
sent me
back
to
work

Unmarked

Novitiate

Don't call me a lite hook. Fluffer. *Sugar baby*
New to the game but born a business lady.
My destiny? One bare speck. Distant shore ...
If I fuck this up, you'll be back. For more.

AK SAINI

Elegy for a Sex Worker Activist
Haibun in Four Seasons

Summer, 2008

My first few months working in the sex industry I learn most of what I need to know using Google and good sense. I want to step up my game, get that white girl money. I learn (also from Google) about a meeting for "sex worker activists."

I arrive at a squat sand-coloured condo complex, the Towne Inn Suites in Southfield, Michigan, where I assume the archaic spelling "towne" of the word "town" signifies to visitors this place is fancy. Or maybe in the context of our meeting Towne referred to Mary Towne Eastey and Rebecca Towne Nurse, sisters executed by their government during the Salem trials for witchcraft. The unit is packed, main and loft floors, with soccer moms and libertarians. I am the only non-white person. I remember I've seen a client here before but I didn't like the space for turning a trick because it was difficult to track what potential threat lurked below, above, around the corner. Now I find myself similarly disconcerted, but there are snacks here, the curated kind found at bourgeois baby showers hosted by suburbanites. I smash a pretty spinach bauble into my mouth, I am starved, I am not yet making enough money to eat consistent.

My voice box blocked with food I respond when asked about my safe-call with a slow shrug and quick head nod back-and-forth, no, I don't have anyone to contact if I get in trouble. I respond with a quick shrug and a slow head nod up and down, sure, I will contact Sarah D if I get in trouble. I do not ask what Sarah D would do if I got in trouble with ICE, police, rapist and I do not think about how they so often travel all three villains in one; I save her number into my burner phone.

Sun rays on sapling
will it to wither or grow
without prejudice.

Autumn, 2011

I bust my ass to get that white girl money, bank stacks, move to New York. I bust my ass to volunteer with a sex worker rights organization. I am one of few non-whites, fewer visible people of colour, this time not soccer moms and libertarians but college students and progressives.

I bust my ass with another volunteer to organize a sex worker film festival. It screens to a sold-out audience. No one except the other volunteer emails me with congratulations on a successful event. Sarah J emails asking if I handed off the profits to the appropriate white girl, which is to say, any white girl. The tone of her email is the same used by an employer talking to a maid trusted alone with the good silverware; whose fault is it, really, when the valuables go missing?

I bust my ass to fix things with Sarah J and the rest. I organize a meeting where we will engage in a conflict resolution process but none of them, Sarah J nor the rest, will attend. I bust my ass to consider where busting my ass with Sarah J and the rest has got me and I cancel the meeting. I bust my ass to maintain my resolve against their drama, delete without reply fuming emails from Sarah J and the rest about cancelling the meeting that Sarah J and the rest never planned on attending.

I bust my ass to get a paid community organizing gig. I bust my ass at that gig. They pay me well, not a lot, and they never send me maid trusted alone with the good silverware toned emails.

Crisp crack of harvest
apple, thrash of reaper scythe,
indiscernible.

Winter, 2015–2016

"I met this unicorn client." It's a cliché worth noting that if not for Sarah P's referral I would dismiss him as too good to be true. A high roller, paying triple or quadruple market rate for multiple overnights with multiple girls at once, within days of each other. I was thirsty for that white girl money.

I refuse to pop the blackheads on his back. His racism works in my favour, at least, he prefers fucking the pink pussy of the other girl to mine. He demands I lick it for him. Since then I tell lovers licking pussy is a sex act I do not perform anymore. I do not explain why I do not perform it anymore and especially not the anymore. In the cab ride home from Jersey the next morning Sarah P texts casually there is a problem at the bank but he is working it out. I reply, wait, you didn't get the money up front? I am almost too exhausted to reply, when she says there was no money up front, that means there is no money at all.

I am not angry at Sarah P just disappointed there is no money, she is incompetent in doing anything about it, and she never musters an apology. I am not angry just disappointed she is subsequently named executive director at the sex worker rights organization I helped build. I am angry not just disappointed when she kicks me out of the organization that I helped build, says they are going in a different direction, I am angry and disappointed at this white girl's attempt to orchestrate my rape again.

I snitch to the board of directors that I believe her actions satisfy the legal definition of sex trafficking and this seems like unbecoming conduct for the incoming executive director of a sex worker rights organization. The board agrees, some of them begrudging with cronyism, she is fired and moves to the opposite coast in shame. The organization and its members splinter.

Pulsating beneath
ice tombed lake persists the tide
beating defiance.

Spring, 2016

In an airport lounge flying back to New York City from a family visit in Toronto I post on the Facebook event page that I will perform my Tale of Two Sarahs. In my seat before takeoff I hear from a friend that all two Sarahs from said Tale, Sarah P and Sarah J, are pitching a fit about my intended performance.

In the customs line on the other end of my flight I learn via the Facebook event page that I was cut from the lineup, a decision made unilaterally by the event organizer, who also claims she is indisposed with a health issue and unavailable for comment or discussion. In a fury I learn that the person deputized to deal with all related comment or discussion, one Sarah S, does not feel herself capable of fielding comment or discussion.

In a haze upon arriving back at my apartment I reach out to some fellow community organizers to ask who might supply me with a bullhorn. In sleep I formulate my plan. In the morning I convince all of my fellow readers to drop out and I recruit supporters to disrupt the performance. In the hopes that I wouldn't have to go through with it, I contact Sarah S to tell her the show will not go on without protest.

In the afternoon the event is postponed indefinitely. In the coming weeks I realize I am done with NYC. In the coming months I move back to Toronto. In the coming years I formally incorporate my hooking business and informally retire from sex worker activism. In time I may return, in the meantime, I get that white girl money.

AK Saini

Naive predator
breaks egg, forgets yolk doubles
as corpse and fetus.

175

Dollymop

> I travelled looking for one,
> or more, discovering:
> in sex shops, libraries,
> in stripper girls, support groups.
> —Trish Salah, "Diagnostic Detour"

Watching *Guys and Dolls* over
Christmas with my sister   it sinks in
I'm Adelaide
      not Jezebel
joke not threat
but Other   either way
a naked model turned clip girl
      wiggling my toes for the camera
      looking for solidarity
in stripper girls' support groups.

We both take our clothes off
for money, right? And   stigma
taints us all
But who am I kidding?
I mostly work in art schools
plausible deniability's veneer
thick as varnish
my escort cred non-existent

I tried to learn the ropes by reading theory
in sex shops   Libraries

that contributed to my own:
      Love for Sale
      Working Sex
      Whores and Other Feminists
As if sex work was easy
      and lucrative
As if all I needed was a website
a shoe size and a few pairs of stilettos
with six-inch heels
or more.   Discovering

that the work *is* easy
but tedious   not lucrative
full of timewasters and attention seekers
I decide I'd rather work a camera
make my money at $2.39 per clip
Even though it takes forever
would still scandalize my mother
and leaves me only a dabbler
No sense of belonging anywhere
I travelled looking for one.

First Time

Six bills
Bank-machine fresh and burning
a hole in their paper sheath
I will always be   current
                      or former
now   Poorly disguised bag of shoes
and cocktail dress I sweated through
slung over my shoulder
three guys in as many blocks   -
tell me I'm pretty
like the first time I fucked
for fun and woke wondering
Where did these curves come from?
I feel unsubtle
unsettled and capable
rent topped up and a day
stretched languid ahead of me
How
are we not all doing this

COURTNEY TROUBLE

Cyborg Dollhouse

little brother.
fag & fuzzy blanket genius artist.
& lesbian eyeballs
& repaired lavender glass jawline & nervous   boy
&
.
disco ball & bunny astronaut
&
smoke robot
asian american femme
talented
grassy
&
stoned &
.
gay
.
&
&
green
&

ISO

like casual reference we found ourselves
3 a.m. wired and wet from the rain
doing something
in a dream state.

. . .

addict domme ISO anymore gold teeth
bitch butch Sir ISO Emotional Swordfighting
feminist cleaning slut lesbian bottom ISO b-o-i Mommy
Lovers, Everywhere.

Fucking for w33d

The moral of this story
is that you should never have sex
for anything other than cold hard cash.

Fucking for love or healthy relationship
will only upset you when it all goes to pieces.

Boys are dumb and
think with their balls.
They will tell you
whatever crap
you want to hear
just so they can ejaculate
in you.

Friends with benefits obliges you in unquantifiable
emotional obligation   dating another sex werker
just means you sign up to alternate being jealous
of each other's actions from all sides
of every transaction.

Fucking for w33d is the kind of crap that weed addicts do.

Clementine

It is dark and warm like my dreams and everyone is perfectly lit and beautiful, a long dining table the wood even darker than the ambience holds a spread of meats and cheese and figs and apples slathered in honey and small lit candles and clementines are scattered around the mismatched plates for décor and I want to shove cloves into the skins of the fruit because I like how the puncture feels under my thumbnail. A figure clad in latex from head to toe stands directly in between two oven lamps in the kitchen and catches my gaze for longer than a moment making me wish my eyes could take photographs, he comes over and pours red wine into fresh lipstick kissed glasses and saunters well in heels and the mood of the room bounces off the lubricated shine of the latex and soon a man who is known for his bite has a snake just as black and shiny as the rubber slut draped around his neck and he tells me to pull back the collar of his T-shirt exposing a tattoo of teeth imprints on his right shoulder and the snake slithers up my hand my arm and it is a long strong muscle flexing and tightening and for a moment I fear constriction around my neck until her perfect shellacked head slick like wet shore rocks comes into sight her black tongue delicate like one single strand of seaweed slips in and out of sight and her tail coils when it falls off my hand and has nowhere to land and Monkey sets up the vacuum bed and rubber slut slides in between the latex sheets and it is loud when turned on and the materials tighten around him constricts like a snake until he is sealed shut in the envelope and Alyx uses the Hitachi wand up and down his enclosed body and the vibration makes him writhe in short sweet movements abrupt and limited and the end of the table has been cleared and doctor has his patient lying down legs spread and two others on each side hold her hands as she moans and screams and groans and I walk around to join the small group of voyeurs and he is suturing her pussy lips pulling the thick thread and needle in and out with large sweeping arm motions with each criss and each cross and my gaze goes back and forth across the dark loft from suction bed to dining table and someone peels open a clementine and the scent is enormous and another passes me the snake as I spit out a cherry pit and then the night really begins.

Jack Slut Session

Jack was a total slut. He would come to session with two bags of groceries: carrots, eggplant, cucumbers, bananas, cherry tomatoes, condoms, wine, cigarettes. He would get naked as we lit up cigarettes and burned his chest hair and nipples making our way down to his ass to mark it with our initials. The room always smelled of singed hair. A light beat down would follow then Jack got down on all fours and we would begin to shove produce up his ass starting with something slender like a carrot and work our way up. He liked to use banana meat as lube, he would get it all mushy between his fingers and rub his cock and taint. We played a game to see how many cherry tomatoes he could hold inside of himself and as we slipped one after the other in he would count them out. When he was too full, some of the cherries would project out of his asshole and we would shove them back and smash them up with the head of a zucchini. After we were finished with his ass, we would piss all over his face. The last time I saw Jack he wanted me to drop liquid cocaine into his eyes with a dropper. That was three years ago.

Buckets

We had a dildo bucket in the dungeon that I made porn at. It was in the bathroom next to the sink. When washing my hands I could look down and see inside. It was filled with water and sanitizer and the dildos would be bobbing up and down, black shiny cocks, beige soft cocks, butt plugs, little purple skinny ones with slim heads for the beginners. I always liked it when is saw the glitter cock in the bucket. It stood out, amongst the other dildos. Most of the girls loved the glitter cock, so it was used often which meant it was always in the bucket. The glitter reminded me of this time I was walking down the street in Chicago in my 20s and I was going through a rough patch likely hungover and as I'm walking down the street I see a sparkly ball on the sidewalk ahead and it caught my eye and as I inched closer so curious to know what it was. It was a beautiful day and the sun was hitting the ball and it was iridescent and glittery and then I was two feet away and it really was brightening my day to see this sparkly ball on the sidewalk and then I was in front of it and that is when I realized it was a pile of dog shit with flies all over it and when the flies flew away and there was no more sparkle and I was admiring a piece of shit.

The gym I worked out at last summer had a puke bucket.

Kelli Lox

1.
taking his thick dick
while eating out her ass
is the sex move, i recall, referred to as "mow'n grass"

2.
Six Dick Bill asked for six whores
i asked why he needed six whores
and Six Dick Bill said
with a nod of his head
for each of my six dicks, of course

3.
now i see it clearly
as my path in life unfurls
that's my claim to fame, i guess
"was good at fucking girls"

I love

My favourite girl was soft, cold
pliable, suggestible
a lumpen sweetheart, with a wall-eyed smile
a cunt of lard, a kiss of butter
We pressed our fat to the cool glass
as white as fresh fish
We listened to the men talk
of fucking our folds
laughing, and we laughed too
Our hands clasped tightly, nails digging into pink flesh
Two hundred for a show of tongues and gasps
and corner shadows, formless grunts
Rinse your bits
Wait for the coarse-skinned woman
red, tough, firm
to take her cut
My girl shortchanged
squeezing into cheap pretty fabric
The pantomime of whores
a sluttish look, the dab of the cloth
at the cum on her dimpled thighs
We sleep, snore, sweat
mingled in each other's life juice
living to be kneaded firmly like dough

DOUG UPP

erik from the park

don't be spooked
by the pox on my cock
I'm still cheap thrill
erik from the park

used to have a little
now I got a lot
when I look below

don't know where they came from

HIMN

Bitch!
Faggots is hot!
One of which
I am not
Butt sometimes I can pass
Get to fuck guys upp the ass

Just strap down my breasts
Strap-on the rest

Over there
Thomas Square
Kapiolani Park
Hell, they can't tell in the dark

Just find some sissy hunk who's all drunk
Or some pissy punk strung out on that junk

In the hanging roots
Of the banyan trees
Force that fool
Down on his knees

And when I say so
He will go
Down on my dildo

Turn him round
And I put it
Right upp his butt

And boys will be boys, hunny
If he wants I'll make noise
What the Hell? I'm pro-choice
Just gotta tone down my voice

When I cum
And we're done
It's no fun.
What can I say?
I'm a bitch
I get attached

Every day I wish
These eggs could hatch
A detachable snatch

Police Brutality

My favorite colors are Blue and White.
My lucky numbers are 9-1-1

So if you wanna get down tonight
whip out your Billy Club
and let's have some fun

Let's play
Police Brutality!
Police Brutality!
Police Brutality!

It's a chance to be close
if you get the nerve
to be just like those
who Protect and Serve

This simple formality's
become a brutal reality
So just sing with the melody
and chant Police Brutality!

Police Brutality!
Police Brutality!
Police Brutality!
There's no need to prove
Unconstitutionality.

Just
Get into the groooooove

And sing
Police Brutality!
Police Brutality!
Police Brutality!

The World's Oldest Love Spell (a Fairy Tale)

True Foxes Massage sat on the corner of 108 Avenue and Whalley Boulevard
and shared a cracked-asphalt parking lot with Triple XXX Adult Video and Toys.

The shop madam bought us quality Jergens brand lotion and Ultra Soft Kleenex®
and baked her trademark double chocolate chocolate chip cookies every Sunday.

Between noon and nine p.m. sugar was the top fragrance note overpowering all
spunk stink and this made Sunday afternoon the most coveted shift on the
    schedule.

We all figured Madam once turned dates herself because who gets DDD
implants for her own entertainment? I greatly favoured True Foxes

over the shop owned by the failed-restaurateur-cum-pimp in Kitsilano
or the shop run by Hells Angels that burned down in a faulty electrical fire.

The only problem with True Foxes was the Surrey RCMP vehicle that often idled
in our parking lot because what date has the nerve to pull up next to a cop car?

We played premises searches right. At the sight of oncoming blues we slipped
into spa robes that covered our bodies between the neck to the top of our knees

and below the elbows. The Body Rub and Lingerie Model Studio licence hung
by the front door in a gold-gilded frame which we routinely tipped from the nail

for inspection. None of our rub rooms were smaller than a cargo van
and all were brighter than fifty candle flames. *You boys think I don't know*

how to run my business? Madam—bless her golden-aged hooker mouth—never
should've back-talked and sure enough the RCMP doubled on us like Doomsday.

Shop will blank if they keep jamming our lot. Fucking cops, they're eating
A&W out there. I got kids to feed. Donna was the one to call the ersatz

stakeout *a curse.* She pinched a ten-spot from her bra. Under the welcome
mat went Sir John A and within the hour we heard the date-doorbell chime.

Whore lore! Why hadn't we thought of it sooner? *Sup-whore-stitious!*
We'd forgotten power but Madam lit the dollar store candles to call a circle.

What charm will we bring? What rue and iron? What divinity and dark?
We salt rimmed the rub rooms and hid rosemary bows under daybeds.

Turn-outs chanted, *money money come to me, in abundance, three times three.*
Golden-agers answered, *harming none on its way, I summon money, come to me.*

Coco rewrote our newspaper ad so each print line added up to numerology nine.
Cleo broke the eyes of six sewing needles. Lily tracked moon cycles. Elle set fires.

We adopted a black cat and named her Willow and for a good long spell
the only blue we saw was the midnight sky as we waved our dates goodbye.

But wind changed again when Donna came late for her shift. *Officer took me*
for a courtesy ride. Bruises rising below each shoulder like she'd been shook.

The following Sunday sparrow flew through the shop window and a plain-clothed cop posing as client followed. He cuffed Cleo before she even toweled him off.

A ready-rolled raid had us stripped to our g-strings for a game of who will cry first. Our purses gutted. Phones wiped. The four corners swept by brute force.

Our stars are un-fixed. Our spring water made ill. We regrouped in the Triple XXX amid the dildos. Madam clanged in anger and avowed, *Ain't no hex*

like a hooker hex. Donna gathered graveyard dirt. Coco knotted black yarn. Cleo summoned Baal. I came flesh-wound close then rethought cutting alms

across my palm. Blood scarification was not made for we who mete out hand jobs as a vocation. Madam turned to her mixing bowl—butter, chocolate chips, spit.

Baneful magic is made worse when cast together. So we gathered round the raw dough. Bitter saliva and tricks on our tongues. *May their might*

overturn. May they be dealt the same hand. May their rule turn to ruin.
May teeth rot from their jaws. May their seeds turn crooked and cruel.

Wait! Lily broke our incantation. *I cursed my father and he went*
mad. Or madder than before. He's moved on to my baby sister now.

Lily's right, said Cleo. *I cursed my first boyfriend and he went*
missing. He's missing still. I wonder about the jerk sometimes.

Coco groaned and swigged back the ritual wine. *Pussy up, witches!*
Cops ought to be taught a lesson. This curse is our duty, our holy charge.

But curses don't teach, curses harm, said Madam. *And harm is hard
to contain, even for sorcery sluts like us. Think wide and wisely.*

We put it to a vote before long our unanimous hands rose. The hex
was nayed. *We still have charm. We can still pussy up,* said Madam.

Her right hand pushed into her panties and we awed. Never before had we seen
Madam uncross her golden-aged legs. We heard polyester lace rip and slush

and then we remembered the oldest of circles. We moaned and wet-messed
in this primordial magic. The spell set as we buried our hands in raw dough.

*We knead passage. We knead respect. We knead love. We knead love.
As below, so above, we knead your love.* The balm of our fresh-baked blessed-

strokes and sugar blew through True Foxes' window and across the parking lot.
Three cop cars rolled in as Madam arranged the warm cookies on a silver tray.

We joined hands as she stiletto-marched out to meet them.
Braced and silent, but chanting *love* behind our teeth.

CONTRIBUTOR BIOGRAPHIES

Aimee Herman is a Brooklyn-based queer performance artist, writer, and teacher with two full-length books of poetry. Aimee's work has been published in a variety of journals and anthologies including *cream city review, BOMB,* and *Troubling the Line: Trans and Genderqueer Poetry and Poetics* (Nightboat Books).

AK Saini is a sex worker and storyteller whose writing appears in various publications including *Feministing,* Bitch Media, *World Policy Journal, Black Girl Dangerous, make/shift,* and the anthology *Dear Sister: Letters from Survivors of Sexual Violence.* Her advocacy work is featured on the cover of *New York Times Magazine,* as well as in an *NYT* documentary short, and throughout the news media including *VICE,* the *Village Voice, Mic, Salon,* the *Daily Beast,* the *Establishment,* and *Marie Claire,* where she was listicled as one of seven sex workers better suited for the presidency than Donald Trump.

Akira the Hustler was born in Tokyo in 1969. He received his BA in 1992 and his MA in 1995, both in oil painting from Kyoto City University of Arts. Akira's project "Living Together Plan" was started to visualize the reality of people living with HIV in 2004. He infuses his work with aspects of his private life, and he is interested in how countercultures can make worlds more attractive. His poetic memoir *A Whore Diary* was first published by Issi Press in 2000.

Alec Butler is a Toronto-based Two-Spirit trans masculine nonbinary playwright, video-maker, performer, and director/curator who was brought up on Cape Breton Island as Audrey. "Lost Fingers" was saved from the fire where they burned most of the dozens of poems they wrote as a queer youth in the early 1970s. Butler is best known for critically acclaimed plays such as *Black Friday?,* which was published in *Lesbian Plays: Coming of Age in Canada* in 2006 and nominated for the Governor General's Award for Drama (English). Alec has contributed articles to *Unwatchable*, a collection of articles by filmmakers, visual artists, and scholars; *Queers Were Here*; and the award-nominated collection *Any Other Way: How Toronto Got Queer*. Alec is pursuing Indigenous Studies and Sexual Diversity Studies at the University of Toronto.

Alili is a South American sex worker living in Europe, whose writing and performance work has appeared in *Sex Worker's Opera*—a multidisciplinary show created and performed by sex workers and friends, devised from stories sent in by sex workers from eighteen countries across six continents. Alilí's poem "When I Crossed the Border" is written for three overlapping voices, bringing together various experiences of underground migration.

Allison Armstrong is a queer, polyamorous leather femme, a kitchen witch, and a Professional Naked Girl, living on unceded Algonquin territory in Ottawa. She has work published or forthcoming in Cuir & Queer Press, Coven Editions, *Bywords.ca*, *Rag Queen Periodical*, *L'Éphémère Review*, *Moonchild Magazine*, and elsewhere.

Amber Dawn Pullin is a wannabe who lives in Toronto. She's kept a journal since she was eleven years old. She loves photography, music, poetry, and reading books. She wants to be a writer.

Arabelle Raphael is an artist, writer, and sex worker living in the Bay Area. Her work ranges from writing, photography, and painting to experimental film. Her work has been featured on *VICE*, KQED, and the *Outline*.

Audacia Ray is a New York–based social justice advocate, storyteller, writer, and editor. She is the author of the book *Naked on the Internet: Hookups, Downloads,* *and Cashing In on Internet Sexploration* (Seal Press, 2007) and an editor of the anthology *$pread: The Best of the Magazine That Illuminated the Sex Industry and Started a Media Revolution* (Feminist Press, 2015). She edited the literary journal *Prose & Lore: Memoir Stories about Sex Work* for three years, publishing stories generated in workshops she led for the Red Umbrella Project, where she was the founding executive director.

Cassandra Blanchard was born in Whitehorse, Yukon, and is part of the Selkirk First Nation. *Fresh Pack of Smokes* is her first book. She resides on Vancouver Island.

Christina V is a freelance writer, journalist, and poet. She thinks the Rolling Stones' *Tattoo You* is the ultimate striptease album.

Courtney Trouble is a writer and artist living in california via the pnw interested in gender, data, and chaos as inspirational topics for works largely informed by the Dada style. they also make semi-autobiographical photographic work and run an indie porn distro, perform and produce porn, and coach other queer sex workers in porn. the poems in this anthology are excerpts from their mfa thesis in studio arts practice entitled *queer chaos/the queen's dictionary.*

Dallas is a white, queer sex worker and self-taught artist working and living on Treaty 1 Territory. Through the exploration and intersecting usages of digital photography, written work, and hand-stitching/sewing, Dallas reflects upon her experiences of sex work, vulnerability, curated persona, and a deep love for femme glamour. Recent works explore autonomy in self-sexualization, the emotional and physical labour of paid seduction, and the right to consensuality and safety for the self-objectified subject. Dallas is currently pursuing a BA in Women's and Gender Studies and allows queer and feminist theory to inform the intentions and meaning behind her work.

Daze Jefferies is an artist-poet-researcher at Memorial University with interests in trans health, sex work, queer archives, and affective ecologies. Her ongoing critical-creative work explores trans-species (fishy) histories, poetics, and subjectivities in Ktaqamkuk/Newfoundland.

Doug Upp is not too deep, and tries to keep grounded. He's found it funner to live in Hawaii, his childhood playground in a parallel paradise. Even though it's the most expensive state to stay alive, his expansive oeuvre has helped him survive as a hometown antihero hasn't-been in his own mind. You won't find his identity in his words, or what you may have heard. But in the hopes of sounding absurd, he's stirred the pot as much as he's smoked it. Stoked less-than-friendly fires, with jokes that have expired, since everyone got woke and higher than mighty on self-righteousness. So Doug hides out in this small pond. Faintly fishy, but fond of the Imminent Riot he incited on the Warped Tour, flexing vocals on the local stage. Totally turning pages out in intermittent zines. Playing in the SF Sex Worker Film Fest, where his mini movie screened. But since seen on public access TV, he's swapped the lipstick-liner-lashes t/v routine, to represent as SWOP-Hawaii co-founder, in some semi femme guy way to identify. Dig Doug on Oahu, in *Manifold Mag*, *Tropic Zine*, *Shaka Talk*, *ThinkTech*, *Contraflow*, and *Ho Stage*.

Exotic Cancer is an artist and stripper from Melbourne, Australia. She has been an artist for all her life and a dancer for the past five years. Her art is heavily influenced by her experience as a dancer, and her subject often reflects the realities of the sex work industry.

Garuda Love was born in Georgia, but currently lives in Los Angeles. She is an MFA candidate at Antioch University and an assistant editor for *Lunch Ticket*. Her writing can be found in *South 85 Journal* and *Recovery Today Magazine*. Garuda was a sex worker from 1991 to 2002, when she worked in Atlanta, New York, San Francisco, San Diego, and LA.

Gregory Scofield is Red River Métis of Cree, Scottish, and European descent whose ancestry can be traced to the fur trade and to the Métis community of Kinosota, Manitoba. He has taught First Nations and Métis Literature and Creative Writing at Brandon University, Emily Carr University of Art + Design, and the Alberta College of Art + Design. He currently holds the position of associate professor in English at Laurentian University where he teaches creative writing, and previously served as writer-in-residence at the University of Manitoba, University of Winnipeg, and Memorial University. Scofield won the Dorothy Livesay Poetry Prize in 1994 for his debut collection, *The Gathering: Stones for the Medicine Wheel*. In addition to several volumes of poetry, Scofield is the author of the memoir *Thunder through My Veins* (1999), and his latest collection of poetry is *Witness, I Am* (2016). In 2016, the Writers' Trust of Canada awarded Scofield with the Latner Writers' Trust Poetry Prize.

Hysterika was given up for adoption at birth and does not know the complete story of her ancestry. She works as a sensual massage therapist providing intimate healing services in the X̱wáy̱x̱way region of Vancouver, while putting herself through school to become a relationship counsellor. She has a black rescue cat and a cherry-red twelve-speed bike.

Irene Wilder is a white settler, full-service sex worker, herb grower, and medicine maker living and working at the confluence of the Speed and Eramosa rivers, on the traditional territory of the Attawandaron, Neutral, and Mississauga of the Credit (Treaty 3) peoples. Her #femmeskills include Lucinda Williams covers and listening closely to the land.

Jaene F. Castrillon is a 2Spirit interdisciplinary artist, activist, author, and award-winning filmmaker who explores her relationship to the world through Indigenous teachings, ceremony, and the wisdom of the land. S/He describes themself as a settler to Turtle Island of mixed heritages (Indigenous Colombian and Hong Kong Chinese) who was adopted as an adult by Elder Isaac Day of Serpent River First

Nation and the teachings of Thunder Mountain. Having survived abuse, institutionalization, homelessness, and sex work, Jaene found herself in Isaac's lodge, where she learned to love and heal. Since then, their journey has been about creating alternative notions around wellness, illness, and worthiness, honouring art as medicine. Jaene believes in sharing the brilliance and heartbreak of living a life less ordinary.

jan maudlin works and writes most recently from unceded Coast Salish territory in Vancouver. Her work has appeared in places such as *Lemonhound*, *Oratorialis*, *Matrix*, *I.D.I.O.T. Magazine*, and PACE Society's *Sex Worker Wisdom* compilation.

Jasbina Justice is an Intersex Femme queer person who is mixed, South Asian, and Caribbean. They are a settler living on colonized land known as Tkaronto, Turtle Island, land of the Haudenosaunee, Anishinaabe, Mississaugas of the New Credit, Huron-Wendat, and other Indigenous peoples. They live with an invisible disability and have complex PTSD. They are a survivor of sexual violence and worked for two decades as a youth and adult sex worker in various areas of the sex industry. They are a poet, writer, multimedia artist, performance artist, sex worker (on hiatus), and yoga teacher.

jaye simpson is a queer indigenous poet who exists in both the spaces of loudly and quietly. they are often disrupting white narratives. they do most of their work in east van cafés. an avid fan of mesh tops, cuffed jeans, and shawls, jaye is often described as witchy & bitchy; they'll drop a house on you and smile whilst doing so.

Juba Kalamka is most recognized for his work with performance troupes Sins Invalid and Mangos With Chili, and as co-founder of the queer hip-hop group Deep Dickollective (D/DC). Kalamka's personal work centres on intersectional dialogues on race, identity, gender, disability, sexuality, and class in popular media. He received a 2005 Creating Change Award from the National LGBTQ

Task Force for his activist work in the queer music community and produced the annual East Bay Pride (Oakland, CA) and sponsored PeaceOUT World Homo Hop Festival from 2002 to 2007, which was featured in the 2005 documentary *Pick Up the Mic*. He regularly appears in queer independent porn features and toured the United States with the Sex Workers Art Show in 2006. In 2015, he attended the White House Bisexual Community Public Policy Briefing with more than forty activists from across the United States. Juba's essays and creative writing appear in numerous journals and anthologies including *Working Sex: Sex Workers Write about a Changing Industry* (2007), *The Yale's Anthology of Rap* (2010), *Recognize: The Voices of Bisexual Men*, and *Queer and Trans Artists of Color: Stories of Some of Our Lives* (2014). He practises polyamory globally and locally.

K.Sedgemore is a former sex worker in both male and Trans sex work. They have provided insight to students and the general public on the reality of Male/Trans sex work as they are often left out of conversions. This has helped influence the work they do now with ARYS (At-Risk Youth Study) as a Peer Research Associate and VCH Peer Harm Reduction leader. Kali advocates for harm reduction and youth harm reduction, and gives talks to different organizations helping people understand youth drug use and youth harm reduction practices. K.Sedgemore is a published poet and writes about their real struggles with addictions and street involvement.

Kay Kassirer (they/them) is a spoken-word poet, organizer, and activist who currently resides on the unceded lands of the Musqueam, Squamish, and Tsleil-Waututh First Nations, colonially known as Vancouver. Kay was the 2016 Capturing Fire rep for Hot Damn! It's a Queer Slam and went on to take second internationally. Kay's work has been featured on *Slamfind*, *Voicemail Poems*, *Write About Now*, and on stages around the world. Using their voice to evoke change, Kay can be found facilitating workshops, organizing poetry events, performing poems, and most likely stuck in a tree.

Kelli Lox is one of the biggest names in the trans porn industry, but her popularity and influence extend far beyond the world of porn. Kelli expresses her creativity in a wide variety of mediums, including poetry, illustration and painting, writing, composing and playing music, and dance.

Keva I Lee is a professional dominatrix, fetish model, and performance artist. Previously, she worked as a counsellor and advocate for sex workers in the criminal justice system, until she decided to become a sex worker herself and never looked back. Keva I Lee first performed in the Sex Workers Art Show 2008, dominating unsuspecting college students across the nation. Since then she has performed at the Sex Workers Fest, Femina Potens, SmackDab, and Desiree Alliance Conference. Her writing and art have been centred on her exploits as an Asian woman working in the kink industry and the constant barrage of stereotypes that come with it. Keva I Lee writes about motherhood, sex, and the challenges of navigating love.

kiran anthony foster is four feet ten inches of in-betweens. an intersex mixed-race queer migrant who's been a sex worker and prison abolitionist all their adult life, they reside in tāmaki-makaurau, aotearoa.

Lavender was born and raised, and lives in the Vancouver area. She is inspired by sex work, emotions, class, drugs, friendship, body image, Vancouver, femininity, intimacy, female artists, imposter syndrome, and the internet. She tries her best to approach these topics with vivid colour and shameless honesty.

Lee-Anne Poole is a Queer writer, arts producer, and the author of seven plays whose work has toured Canada and Europe. Her first full-length play, *Splinters*, has been adapted into a feature film.

Lester Mayers is a Brooklyn native who is currently completing his undergraduate degree in theatre performance at SUNY New Paltz School of Fine and

Performing Arts. Lester is a published writer, poet, and actor. In 2017, Lester won the SUNY Chancellor's Awards for Artistic Excellence. His work can be found in the Sojourner Truth Library, I am from Driftwood LGBTQ archive, and the *Huffington Post.* Lester has survived homelessness and abuse, has pried his self loose of illiteracy, and performs nonstop diversity work.

Lorelei Lee is a sex worker and writer. Her fiction, non-fiction, and poetry have appeared or are forthcoming in *Salon,* the *Rumpus, WIRED, Denver Quarterly,* the *Los Angeles Review of Books,* the *Establishment, Buzzfeed, $pread Magazine, 1111, The Feminist Porn Book, Coming Out Like a Porn Star,* and elsewhere. She owes her life to other sex workers.

Marcelle Nuke is a student, escort, and campaigner based in Edinburgh, Scotland. Marcelle has worked in the British sex industry since the age of nineteen, which partly aided in developing her political consciousness and led to her studying politics and sociology with a focus on neoliberalism and its atomising effects. An aspiring writer, she can be found on Twitter at @whoraura, and has a podcast, *Rules of Conduct,* with journalist Robert Somynne.

Mélodie Nelson thinks tiaras are the best accessory for any occasion. She has been a topless waitress, phone sex operator, webcam girl, and escort. She is a writer for *VICE* Québec and has published *Escort Girl* (2010) and *Juicy* (2017). She tells her kids that she will never die and she doesn't know if it's good or bad. Her feet are ugly, but her ass makes up for that.

Mercedes Eng writes and makes text-based art in Vancouver, on the unceded territories of the Musqueam, Squamish, and Tsleil-Waututh Nations. She is the author of *Mercenary English,* a long poem about violence and resistance in the Downtown Eastside neighbourhood of Vancouver, and *Prison Industrial Complex Explodes,* winner of the 2018 Dorothy Livesay Poetry Prize. Her writing has appeared in *Jacket 2*, *The Downtown East/Volcano*, and the collectively produced chapbooks *r/ally*, *Surveillance*, and *M'aidez*.

Milcah Halili (they/he) is a nonbinary writer, web developer, and performer. They write about intersectionality, cannabis, sexuality, and web development. They've been published in *Coming Out Like a Porn Star*, *Witch Craft Mag*, the *Rumpus*, and *Filthy Media*. He lives in Los Angeles with his wife, April Flores.

Miss Sugar Mamasota is an interdisciplinary artist, burlesque performer, and nude model. In her recent travels abroad, Miss Sugar wrote a series of poems addressing bodily autonomy and recovery from trauma and disassociation.

Moon Dancer is the nom de plume for the sex worker known to her clients as Diva, who lives and works in St. John's, Newfoundland. She lives with her partner of eleven years, "Lion," who is also a sex worker. She has aspirations of one day becoming a successful full-time author/writer and has several projects she is working on.

Naomi Sayers is a fierce Indigenous feminist, influencer, writer, and educator. An Indigenous lawyer, she is passionate about working with Indigenous communities or organizations with an Indigenous focus. Naomi enjoys using her life experiences to inspire others to make change possible in their world. Naomi is Kwe behind *Kwe Today*, a blog that is regularly cited around the world. Her work is also used by national and international organizations to influence policy and law reform. She was the only First Nations woman with lived experience to oppose former prime minister Stephen Harper's bill in response to *Canada v Bedford*, in which Canada's highest court held three prostitution provisions as invalid for violating sex workers' protected Charter rights. Naomi is very grateful to be able to use her lived experiences to advocate for change in the lives of Indigenous sex workers around the world.

Natalie House is a twenty-two-year-old university student studying to become a social worker. Their identity as a gay young person has helped shape their poetry; themes of religion and the mystic often inform their writing. Their goal is to have their work published and to achieve their dreams of helping others through support and social work.

Natasha Gornik has been involved in sex work as a Pro-Domme/pornographer/photographer since 1995. She began writing about her experiences with kink, in both lifestyle and profession, in 2009. Her life's work has been focused on her exploration into intimacy. She was born in Chicago and lives in Brooklyn.

Pluma Sumaq is a poet, writer, and photographer. A two-time VONA fellow, she is the recipient of a Poets 11 award and the creator of a chapbook of poetry by people in the sex trade titled, *Places of Eclipse*. Her article "A Disgrace Reserved for Prostitutes: Complicity & The Beloved Community" was published in *LIES, Volume II: A Journal of Materialist Feminism*. Her writing has appeared in *The Body Is Not an Apology*, and she's recently completed a writing residency at Hedgebrook. Having grown up on the border of Harlem and Washington Heights in New York, as well as in between Ecuador and the Dominican Republic, her work is largely influenced by a lived experience of magical realism. She lives in California and is working on her first book, in a genre that is yet to be determined.

Raven Slander is originally from Tiohtià:ke (Montreal), and has travelled North America's highways East Coast, West Coast, and across. She writes and performs her work about her lived experiences, chronicling her early life of sex work, addiction, treachery, and love, giving voice to the disappeared, the dispossessed, and the darkness. Residing on the traditional Coast Salish territory of the Musqueam, Tsleil-Waututh, and Squamish First Nations (Vancouver), Raven advocates for transgender justice and services and continues to learn from and contribute to the queer/trans writing community.

Rhanimalz is a Los Angeles-born sparkly rascal who currently plays music, draws, and writes in the Bay Area. She loves thrifting, the smell of gardenias, freestyle music, and cats. She would rather be a truck driver than a nurse. Sun in Scorpio, Moon in Sagittarius. Down for creative collaborations that embrace the weird.

Sacred Collective is an Indigenous sex worker group based out of Peers Victoria—a multi-service grassroots agency sex worker resource centre on the unceded territories of the Songhees and Esquimalt people.

Sascha is a queer writer, health care activist, and organizer with SWOP-Los Angeles. Her work can be found in *Playboy*, *VICE*, *SELF*, the *Washington Post*, and other publications.

Stickie Stackedhouse was born on Tsleil-Waututh territory, raised poor and happy by closeted gays and whores. Hustling really boring dads since 2005. Full service #ftp and the whorearchy. Stickie Stackedhouse loves her cat and other fems and learning what stability feels like.

Strawberry is an escort, punk, partner, writer, and mischief-maker located on Vancouver Island. They are a nonbinary recovering addict who loves cats and hates capitalism.

Summer Wright is a trans woman who survived the first half of young adulthood through poetry and sex work. She currently lives in England and the USA.

Sumter is a multi-amorous storyteller, photographer, and filmmaker who is an eighth-generation Black Canadian with Mi'kmaq, Cherokee, and Scottish ancestry born in Winnipeg and now living in Vancouver on unceded Coast Salish Territory. Sumter identifies as Queer, gender nonbinary, and in the absence of direct knowledge of original culture is left here questioning. Work here has been in support of community, and for Sumter art and writing is more private and anchored in intimate expression.

SybilLamb.com has been paying for art supplies with sex and sex supplies with art for so long she can't tell the diff anymore. she's kinna famous cuz she wrote a notorious trans punk violence sex-change drugs 'n' rock 'n' roll novel *I've Got a Time Bomb*, but her number one passion is drawing cartoons and selling them as fine art around Southern Ontario. She is available most evenings within thirty minutes notice.

Tracy Quan is the author of three novels, including *Diary of a Manhattan Call Girl*, narrated by a duplicitous Ottawa runaway. Tracy's juvenile career began in lobby bars and hostess clubs, with Times Square and the Pierre hotel playing equally prominent roles. Inspired by an international gathering of sex workers held in Ann Snitow's New York loft, Tracy joined PONY (Prostitutes of New York), chaired a few meetings, and was, for a brief time, its token conservative. Tracy's essays have been published in the *Globe and Mail, Marie Claire*, the *New York Times*, the *Washington Post Book World*, the *Financial Times, Der Tagesspiegel*, the *South China Morning Post*, the *Guardian, Bookanista*, and the *Daily Beast*. Tracy's poetry has appeared in *Poets Reading the News* and the *Los Angeles Review of Books*.

tzaz is an interdisciplinary artist, writer, and sex worker who cares deeply about bodies. They are a proud founding member of a queer sex work collective. tzaz performed at documenta 14 and is a 2018 Lambda Literary Fellow, among other things.

X. Rae Alessandro is a New England–based full-service sex worker. Disabled, queer, and trans, Rae has an intersection of sexual interests with a focus on decolonizing sexuality and making it accessible. Their sexuality has grown and developed over their years of doing sex work, and they continue to explore new and weird fetishes. They have a wide variety of hobbies, including gaming, watching sci-fi movies, and doing elaborate makeup routines.

ACKNOWLEDGMENTS

Like sex work justice itself, *Hustling Verse* is a collaborative effort that has been uplifted by supporters who are not represented within these 218 pages. Many sex workers, and sex worker and allied organizations, inspired us, mentored us, and helped spread the word about *Hustling Verse* during the past two years.

Love to Rachel Rabbit White, Afuwa Granger, Vixen Noir, Sarah Hunt, Shane Sable, Jónína Kirton, Jamie Lee Hamilton, Nahshon Dion Anderson, and Arielle Twist.

Respect and appreciation to our poetry-loving and sex work justice–minded allies: the League of Canadian Poets, Read Local BC, *Room* magazine and Indigenous Brilliance, the *Capilano Review*, the *TransForming Rounds* trans-competent health care podcast, Venus Envy Halifax, and Lambda Literary.

Deepest gratitude to our unstoppable friends at *by us, for us* sex worker organizations across Canada: the Sacred Collective, Peers Victoria Resource Society, PACE Society, Sex Workers United Against Violence (SWUAV), SWAN Vancouver, Sex Workers of Winnipeg Action Coalition, Monica Forrester and Maggie's Toronto, and Bridget and the Safe Harbour Outreach Project team in St. John's, Newfoundland. And also to our international friends Juba Kalamka and the St. James Infirmary in San Francisco, Caty Simon and the *Tits and Sass* blog, Jane Green and the Vixen Collective in Melbourne, Australia, and the EMPOWER Foundation in Thailand.

Finally, a special thank you to the Sex Worker's Opera. The team at this multidisciplinary, collaborative project shared resources, wisdom, and stories that helped us shape *Hustling Verse*. To read more creative and varied sex work stories, we recommend visiting their online global story collection at *sexworkersopera.com/stories*.

Sarah Race photography

JUSTIN DUCHARME is a filmmaker, writer, dancer, and curator from the small Métis community of St. Ambroise in Treaty 1 Territory. He is a graduate from Vancouver Film School and the writer/director of three short narrative films. He has been jigging since the age of seven, performing with the St. Ambroise Youth Steppers and the Louis Riel Métis Dancers. His poetry has been featured in *Sex Worker Wisdom* and *PRISM international* magazine. He lives and works on unceded Coast Salish Territory.

AMBER DAWN is the author of the novels *Sodom Road Exit* (2018) and *Sub Rosa* (winner of a Lambda Literary Award, 2010); the Vancouver Book Award–winning *How Poetry Saved My Life: A Hustler's Memoir* (2013); and the Dorothy Livesay Poetry Prize–nominated collection *Where the words end and my body begins* (2015). She teaches creative writing at Douglas College in Vancouver and leads several low-barrier community writing classes.